I0151136

Kopek the Destroyer

Causes of indigestion for a wolfy puppy

By

Phil Owens

This Second edition was published in the UK in 2015 by Kopek Publishing. – Grammatical and vocabulary changes only

ISBN: 978-0-9561496-0-2

NOTE: This is a work of fiction, in so far as the author cannot remember the exact details regarding some of the episodes. Some of the names of people and animals have been changed to protect the guilty.

For my wonderful wife.
Without whose amazing
understanding I would
probably be bereft of
dogs.

Contents

Prologue...1

Chapter 1 - The growing family..........................3

Chapter 2 - The puppy arrives.......................23

Chapter 3 - The first few months 41

Chapter 4 - The next few months....................61

Chapter 5 - The escapologist..........................83

Chapter 6 - I haven't killed him yet..................99

Chapter 7 - Out and about 113

Kopek's Story in Pictures.............................129

Acknowledgments

I would like to thank my wife first and foremost as without her encouragement this book would never have been completed. Her patience in reading draft after draft was a wonderful gift.

I would also like to thank friends and family, who have allowed me to put into print, some of their experiences with Kopek. Also, their patience with me, for continually changing the draft that they helped proofread. I would also like to say a big thank you to those on the YouWriteOn website, especially Chris Pitt, whose reviews of my sample chapters were invaluable.

Finally, I would like to thank all those wonderful animals, including Kopek, without which our lives would be so much duller.

Prologue

"Oh no, not again," these were the words that came to mind the minute I opened the front door. There, as far as the eye could see were hundreds of chewed up pieces of toilet roll. A thin layer of Andrex Super Soft completely covered the hall and stairs.

My wife had returned the night before from doing the weekly shop on her way home from work. Ever the one to keep an eye on the pennies, she was extolling the virtues of shopping for a bargain.

"Look, I saved nearly a pound by buying a twenty-four-pack rather than the usual four-pack."

"How many of us live here?" I asked her.

"Two," she replied.

"And how many rolls do we go through in a week?"

"Two," she mumbled. She already knew where I was going with this.

"Mmm, twenty-four rolls at two rolls a week, at least they won't go off. So what should we do with this week's eight pence you've saved?"

"How about we go to the pub?"

"Get your coat, at least if I overdo it on the Guinness, there's enough toilet roll," I said laughing. (If you drink Guinness, you will know what I mean).

"You little bugger!" I shouted at the dog, and what was a happy tongue lolling face suddenly did a handbrake turn, and shot down the hall, leaving a blizzard of white toilet roll flying in the air behind him. He only stopped when he thought there was a safe distance between us. Kopek was standing legs wide apart, halfway down the hall, with his head on one side. He seemed to be unsure whether to make a run for safety or jump into my arms for a cuddle.

Decision made; he turned and ran, creating a bow wave of Andrex as I chased him into the kitchen. Kopek jumped, madly pawing the kitchen door handle. Success, he shot out into the back garden as if there were a dozen gerbils gnawing at his tail. After hurling one last vociferation after him, I locked the door and started to survey the size of the clean-up job. Tiny strips of toilet paper, all about 1-inch square and a lot of it still soggy with dog saliva, completely covered the kitchen, the hall, the stairs, the landing, and even the bedroom. Of the original twenty-four rolls, there was but one half-mangled damp one left, my coming home just as he was finishing that one off had obviously interrupted him. I hadn't owned a puppy for a long time and had forgotten just how much hard work they were. We had bought this puppy two months previously, and we were starting to wonder whether we were completely sane when we made this decision. The puppy was a replacement for the hole left in our lives after our previous dog had left us for the big field in the sky.

Chapter 1 - The growing family

Two rabbits, a dog, another rabbit, yet another rabbit, then a cat. It was starting to feel like the ark.

To understand how and why we ended up with this wonderful destructive ball of fur with long floppy legs, it's necessary to go back to when my then future wife and I first started dating. We had both met late in life, in our mid to late thirties (that is she was 'mid,' and I was 'late'). Apart from some very brief periods, I had always had at least one dog in my life. However, Ronnie at that time was very much a rodent person or more specifically, she was into lagomorphs. No, this was not some form of sexual deviancy. As rabbits are not strictly of the rodent family, this is the correct name for them. Of course, we simply referred to them as rodents, for us this was a term of endearment; although I'm not too sure how happy they were about this. Ronnie had no experience of keeping any other type of animals, except rabbits and guinea pigs.

When we first met, it was one of those brief periods in my life in which I was without a dog. However, Ronnie had two rabbits she had adopted from a rescue centre in Essex. Being an aficionado of 1970s films, she had named them Donald and Elliot, after Donald Sutherland and Elliot Gould. Despite the oddness of this naming convention, it was a vast improvement on her previous rabbit's name; she had called that one Brown Bun. Now I love all types of animals, especially ones with fur on. However, I had never gone in for rodents too much, as I wasn't sure how much they gave you back. I did learn to love those two rabbits though.

Actually, I did have a rodent once. I had a hamster called Miss Otis (as in Miss Otis regrets, the title of a song some older readers might remember), but I was not overly impressed with her. Apart from doing a Tarzan impression along the top of her cage, she didn't do too much as far as entertainment value went. If anything, she was a real pain in the butt. Once she had learned how to open her cage, she was always escaping. Otis had her cage in the box-room, and there was many a time I had to spend hours searching, making sure that I hadn't left the door open lest she escaped into the main house. Searching for a hamster is not the easiest task in the world at the best of times. I had to make sure that anything I lifted up, I did so very carefully, just to make sure no squishing occurred. She once disappeared for three days, and, to be honest; I thought she had escaped out of the box-room, and I would never see her again. It was only when my printer stopped working I found where she had disappeared to. She had managed to worm her way inside and build a nest inside of it. She had nibbled all the internal wiring, and it was a small wonder she didn't electrocute herself. I had to take the printer apart to get her out and then had to go and buy another printer. Thinking about it, this episode did nothing to endear me to rodents, and it's probably the reason I never got another one.

Now rabbits are not without their quirks, such as the time Ronnie thought all her friends had sent her to Coventry. It was only when she discovered that three days previously one of her rabbits had taken a fancy to her telephone line, and eaten about two foot of it. She then understood why nobody had rung her for so long. Then there was the time she had some friends round for dinner, only for one of her guests to fall through the seat of the chair. Unfortunately, one of the rabbits had taken a liking to the raffia making up the seat and had pretty much chomped its way through it.

Ronnie had made up for her rabbit's lack of personality by inventing a fantasy life along with a language for her rodents. Rabbits were known as 'booners,' and guinea pigs were referred to as 'pigglies.' She had even extended these names to other furry rodents like squirrels; these took n the moniker of 'squirlies.' The collective name for all these animals was 'rodentia' as in some sort of mafia-style family. In her mind, when she was out at work, she could quite happily picture her rabbits playing poker, watching the television, and getting up to all sorts of mischievous things. I wouldn't want you to get the impression that she is completely crazy, but she certainly has an extremely fertile imagination.

There was one time when I had lost patience with Donald; it was while I was trying to get him into his hutch for the night. He refused to co-operate, and I ended up prodding him in the rear end with a bamboo cane. Ronnie admonished me saying, "If you're not careful, you'll get a visit from the Rodent Council. They don't take too kindly to that sort of thing." This council was an imaginary group of animals that looked after the interests of all rodents, and according to Ronnie, they also enforced the rodent law. Apparently, if any rodents were caught stealing carrots from the local Co-Op, the Rodent Council would sentence them to a punishment of some sort. This punishment was generally community service; cleaning up the fallen acorns from the park, or some such thing. This imagination was not limited to live furry animals. We have an enormous collection of stuffed toy animals, every one of which Ronnie has named, allocated an occupation and a complete life full of activities. For instance, there was Merv' the Magician, a furry white bear with a black top hat, whose hobbies included stamp collecting and was a member of CAMRA. All this was as well as performing magic tricks of course. Mmmm, thinking about it, I think Ronnie may well be certifiable, but then, as I enjoy playing with imagination so much I'm probably just as barking mad.

My future wife and I had dated for a couple of years before we made the big decision to get married. A year prior to the wedding, we decided to move out of the rented house that we shared, and start looking for a property to buy. We spent a few months hunting for just that perfect house, one that ticked all the boxes. Finally, we found our new home, a decent sized semi-detached property, in a large town in Suffolk. We bought it for a very good price at the time, but it was a bargain for a reason. While there was nothing structurally wrong, it did need some major cosmetic renovation. It was a three bedroomed 1930s house, so it had large rooms with high ceilings, and a seventy-foot garden with a garage at the end of it. Every single wall needed at least painting, and a few needed a good skim over with fresh plaster. Apart from the lounge, every floor needed something doing with it. So, we decided to carpet the hall, stairs, and landing, then sand-down and varnish the rest of the floors. The one thing that made this house such a good one for me was that it had a dining room. As the lounge was almost 30-foot-long, we could put a dining table in there, so this meant that I could convert the dining room into my big boy's playroom.

To say Ronnie is house proud is a slight understatement. She is not as extreme as to enforce living in a show-house environment, but cleanliness and tidiness are never far from her mind. My attitude to housework is typically mannish, 'there's always room for one more plate in the washing up bowl.' I always have to be careful I don't leave anything lying around for any length of time unless I have finished with it. Or else she'll whisk it off, clean it, and put it away; even if it's my unfinished mug of coffee. There are common conversations between us that go along the following lines.

"Fancy a cup of coffee hon?" Ronnie would ask

"No thanks, I haven't finished the one in my room."

"Ah, I'll get you a fresh one."

"You did it again, didn't you."

"Sorry."

With her eye for neatness and her desire for everything to be 'just right,' it took us nearly six months to bring the house up to a condition that she would be happy living in. I say 'she' as her standards are considerably higher than mine, and I'd be happy living in a much less tidy house. We could have finished a lot sooner, but we did most of the work ourselves apart from the electrics. I only touch electric in emergencies as I'm colour-blind. This has resulted in some rather interesting results from my tinkering. The kitchen with its very nice original quarry tiles on the floor came up a treat, but the tired old cupboards, which while not perfect, we felt we could live with for a while. Apart from being small, the bathroom was fine, and as there was only the two of us we thought it would keep as it was for the time being. These two rooms were the only ones we did little work on, the rest needed a major overhaul. I think those six months were the hardest I had worked for a long while. I'm not averse to physical labour, but I tend to go a long way to try to avoid it. No, actually truth be told I am extremely averse to physical labour, and my idea of exercise is walking to the car, lifting pints, or if absolutely necessary walking home from the pub.

When we had finally finished work on the house, and everything was in its proper place, it was not long before the subject of getting a dog came up. "You know what's missing in the house?" I said. "A dog?" Ronnie answered. Perhaps I hadn't been quite as subtle as I had thought. I had been dropping, what I considered were, obscure hints for the last couple of months, about how much I missed having a dog. "Well, actually, that's exactly what I was thinking." Because she had never had a dog before, Ronnie was understandably a little apprehensive. However, with her being such a big an animal lover, it didn't take too much to convince her. As it would be her first time, my thoughts had been to get an older dog, maybe a three or four-year-old. House training a puppy can be a long and painful experience, and with an older dog, this shouldn't be necessary. I was not sure how my house-proud wife would take to a puppy messing up her nice clean floors, irrespective of how cute it was. Perhaps we could even find one with a quiet demeanour, and one that already had some basic training so it would be fairly easy to look after. I knew this was probably asking too much, but I was ever hopeful. A ready trained dog would help to ease Ronnie into the canine ownership club without too much upset to the easy routine, and cleanliness of the house.

After a bit of discussion, with me telling Ronnie what we should be looking for and why, we decided we would first look into getting a dog from a rescue centre. As we are both very sentimental as far as animals go, we wanted to give a rejected dog another chance at a happy life. There is a Blue Cross animal rescue centre in Felixstowe, which is not too far from where we live, so we thought we'd try there first. Arriving at the centre one Saturday afternoon, a cacophony of dogs howling and barking had us quite excited. We went up to the main desk and told the woman sat behind it that we were looking to adopt a dog. A few minutes later, we were shown into an interview room. The manageress then started asking us questions as to what we were looking for.

After listening to our requirements, the manageress said, "I don't think we have any dogs in that are exactly what you are looking for. But, as you have a lot of experience with rescue dogs, there is one I think you would make perfect owners for." Our heads, which had been dropping at that point, lifted up with interest. She proceeded to pour out such a sob story that we were both nearly in tears at the end. "He was brought in almost eighteen months ago. Unfortunately, his owners were splitting up, and neither could keep him. He wasn't in a very good state I'm afraid, and he's taken a lot of patience to get him to trust us." She explained, "Once, we did manage to find him a lovely home, but he wouldn't get on with the adopter's other dog, so we had to take him back after only a month." She then started to extol the virtues of Tim.

"He's such a lovely old chap, very docile, but needs lots of love."

"He's house trained, and knows quite a few commands."

"He's also used to being left on his own, so he won't be any trouble with regards to that."

"There is one problem we have with him, and that is he doesn't really get on with the other dogs and tends to bark at them all day. That's the reason he's kept in my office, but he should be perfectly happy if he's the only dog in the house."

What a sell job, I tell you the manageress of the Blue Cross could have made a fortune selling shoes to dolphins. She knew exactly which strings to pull on our hearts, and by this point, we were well and truly suckered, we couldn't wait to see poor old Tim. She then led us to her office, and we were introduced to an eleven-year-old scruffy grouch of a Border Collie. Now don't start feeling sorry for Tim, because this old grouch was nobody's fool. I think because he had been around the block a few times he was able to put on such a sweet front. This was how Tim had somehow managed to wrangle his way into living in the manageress' office. This meant that he received special treats and lots more attention than the other dogs. He graciously allowed us to pet him, tickling his ears, and giving his tummy a rub, all with no sign of what was to come in the very near future.

The Blue Cross has certain rules that prospective adopters need to comply with before an animal can be taken home. One of these is they have to take the dog that they think they might want for at least two walks. We had both fallen for Tim, so much so that we took him for those two walks that same week. Tim had been at the centre for so long, and so many people had walked him so many times, he knew the route off by heart. When we arrived for the first session, he pretty much took us for a walk. He seemed such a nice quiet dog and was no trouble at all during those walks. When in the middle of the second one, we sat down to have a chat about whether he was the right dog for us; he sat quietly near us simply snuffling his nose into the grass. It didn't take long for us to make up our minds, and decide that Tim was the dog for us. So, after finishing the walk, we arranged for him to come home with us the following week. This would be after a home visit by the centre, to check on the suitability of our house and garden for Tim.

Although I would have no hesitation in recommending the Blue Cross, I would have to give a word of warning if you ever intend to go there looking for an animal to adopt. And that is to be very careful to try to avoid the manageress. Otherwise, you will end up with what she thinks is the best match, irrespective of what type of animal you went there to get, and that may not be quite what you were expecting. However, I do have to say, the manageress was spot on, Tim was the perfect dog for us, and we would not have swapped him for anything.

We loved Tim with all our hearts, but he was an awful lot of hard work in the first year of his life with us. He was such a bad-tempered grouch, and he did not like strangers in the house at all. During that first couple of months, he managed to bite each and every one of our friends. He didn't have a nasty bite, but one of those nips that just pinched your skin with his front teeth, and then left a large bruise. It was a testament to how good our friends were that they carried on not only speaking to us but also continuing to come round. Most of our friends soon took to bringing large supplies of dog treats with them when they called, they would then slowly feed these treats to Tim while chatting away. When the treats finished, so did the visit. I think it was a hard call for Tim whether to go in for a nip or eat the treat. The indecision was written all over his furry face, "shoe, or food? Shoe, or food? I suppose I can always take the food and go for the shoe later." Luckily for us, and our friends, the food won out more often than not, but not always.

Believe me, Tim didn't spare us the nipping, and some days my legs were a mixture of blue, yellow, and black, from the bruising of his ministrations. Tim would try to stop either of us leaving the house through the front door by continuous circling round our legs. He would dart in with a sharp nip for encouragement; it was as though he was trying to herd us back into the house. It took almost a year of hard work and patience, to give him the confidence that we were going to keep him and not send him back to the Blue Cross. He did eventually learn that we didn't need herding with nips, although he never did stop completely. But, I think this was just to keep us on our toes and keep his hand in. On the subject of grouchiness, there was only one person Tim never nipped, and unbelievably, that was the mother in law. We never could quite understand this. Did this mean that he liked her? On the other hand, was it perhaps that he was just as afraid of her as the rest of us?

Tim turned out to be the perfect dog to introduce my wife to the joys of canine ownership. He was such a great dog, with a unique character and outlook on life. Ronnie grew to love and appreciate just what it was to have a dog as part of the family. It was during this period we came to know our local Pets at Home store very well. What with dog food for Tim, and feed and hay for the rabbits, we tended to spend a fair bit of time there. When it comes to furry animals, I have to admit I am a total sucker. I just cannot resist touching, stroking, or playing with them, and Pets at Home is a perfect place to satisfy this affliction. However, I'm also rather impulsive, and this along with my love of animals is a dangerous combination. I really should never be allowed to go to a pet shop on my own. You know those signs that read 'All children must be accompanied by a responsible adult.' Well in my case, they should read 'Do not enter unless you are feeling responsible today.'

It was because of this combination of impulsiveness and love of animals that we ended up with another addition to the family. One day, I was out shopping at Pets at Home for the usual animal supplies, when I passed the enclosure for the rabbits and guinea pigs that they have for sale. I could not resist having a peek in. Bad move, very bad move. There on one side of the enclosure was the sorriest looking black rabbit you were ever likely to see. He was all on his own, with no friends to play with or keep him company. That was it, how could I leave him there.

I stood in the store for a good fifteen minutes deliberating. "Should I, shouldn't I? Should I, shouldn't I?" Well, I crumbled. I couldn't bear the thought of him there all on his own, especially at night, so fifteen minutes later I was back in the car with a small cardboard box containing a rabbit. As I was driving home, it slowly dawned on me that Ronnie just might have some objection to a new rabbit. I desperately started to think of what excuse could I possibly come up with to explain what had happened. By the time I had driven up to the house, I had discounted all the reasons I could think of as being either a) implausible, or b) just not logical. I realised there wasn't much I could say that would make sense, so I was going to be grown up, and simply go in and announce that I had decided to buy another rabbit.

When I entered the house, I put the cardboard box on the kitchen table and went into the lounge to see Ronnie, who was stretched out on the couch, reading a book.

"What do you think is a good name for a rabbit?" I asked

"What do you mean?" she asked, with a confused frown

"Well, if we were to get another rabbit, what would you call it?"

"That depends; I think I'd have to see it first. Where is this going?" She asked. The wrinkles on her forehead had deepened; this was not a good sign.

"Err... Well..., I may have done something a bit daft." It was time to come clean and own up to what I had done. "Come and have a look." I tried to put my innocent face on.

"Oh, he's lovely," cooed Ronnie. "But how come we've got him?"

"I just couldn't help it, it's not my fault" I whined. Out came a story of how miserable he looked, and how all the guinea pigs were ganging up on him.

"They were extorting carrots from him," I exclaimed. "They were making him pay protection." I had started to get on a roll.

"And..., and..., and he'd run out of carrots, and they were going to beat him up tonight, so I just had to get him out of there before it was too late." A masterpiece of storytelling I thought. I was quite sure she didn't believe me, but she was sympathetic. As she loved this sort of story, and this was the first time I had done anything like this, she gave me an odd look, but let it go.

"Well, what are we going to call him?" I asked, hoping the deal was done.

"How about Steve McQueen?" she said, and that was that.

It was pretty much the same story concerning Wayne, the guinea pig. This time, she was not quite as understanding, or sympathetic, and, to be honest, the story was not quite as good the Steve one. However, as she feels the same as me when it comes to furry animals, she soon came round, and we made accommodation for Wayne. Wayne was named after John 'The Duke' Wayne, one of my childhood heroes, it's sad I know. This impulsive behaviour of mine has resulted in Ronnie always being on tenterhooks whenever I venture out alone to anywhere where there may be furry animals, of any kind. Usually, she wouldn't let me go to Pets at Home alone, or indeed anywhere where there might be furries. However, there was the odd occasion when she didn't have a choice but to let me go and take a chance. Still, I'm not the one who nearly bought a goat from the local farm. I still like to remind her of that sometimes.

Left to Right – Donald, (a small furry toy, Pip), Elliot, and Wayne hiding behind Elliot

One morning, when I went to give the rodents their food in the hutch, I found Elliot lying on his side. It looked like he had passed away overnight, it seemed as though he had gone quietly in his sleep, and I was thankful for that at least. Ronnie was very upset. She had had Elliot for several years and had grown very attached to him, and to my surprise, so had I. Obviously, we had to get another rabbit; I don't think we even discussed getting one or not. It was a no-brainer of a decision really if only to keep Donald and Wayne company. Well, just Donald really, as Wayne was a grumpy old so and so, almost as bad as Tim.

We had discovered a rabbit rescue centre close by to where we lived. So rather than go to Pets at Home, we thought we would go and visit to see what they had available. The centre had many rabbits, guinea pigs too, but Ronnie wanted another rabbit, so the pigs were out. This was a shame, as I had quite taken to guinea pigs, generally being grumpy things I found I could empathise with them somewhat. Anyway, a rabbit it had to be. Enter Ali McGraw. Ali was a pure white rabbit, who took to the rest of the family within a short period, and she soon settled into the family routine. We had somehow now accumulated three rabbits, a guinea pig, and Tim. Quite a growing family, but it did not stop there.

One day, a good friend of ours called Chris asked me to help him move his daughter between flats. Chris was one of my oldest friends from Suffolk, and he was my drinking buddy. So, when he asked for help, despite my natural aversion to physical labour, I, of course, said yes. We set off mid-morning to get to the flat his daughter was moving out of. When we arrived, Chris began to organise things; he started to sort the boxes in the order that we would be moving them. Chris is a great organiser, a lot better than I am, so I left him to it and had a wander around the flat.

There in the corner of the lounge was the cutest kitten I had ever seen sitting in her pink travel box. Of course, I couldn't resist and was over to the box like a shot. She looked so cute, and at the same time miserable in her little pink prison.

"Who's this?" I called out to Chris.

"That's Gucci," He said, "I know, a really awful name, but then that's my daughter. She likes the finer things in life you know," He laughed.

His daughter then came into the lounge, and she was quite upset because the flat she was going to didn't allow animals. She said that as Gucci couldn't go with her, she was going to have to take her to the RSPCA.

Now I have the utmost respect for the RSPCA, they do a lot of fantastic work for animals in need, but I do have a problem with some of their rules. Sometimes some of the rules seem to be a bit on the extreme side, and they will not bend them for anyone, or any circumstances. I once read a story in the paper regarding the vet at one of the RSPCA centres. He had half a dozen dogs I think, and when one passed away, he asked if he could take one of the rescue dogs home. The centre refused, as they would not allow more than one male dog in the same home, this was despite the fact that he already had more than one male dog. This was the same vet that they went to for advice on re-homing their animals! Now I know there are probably good reasons for this, but surely, it would be better to evaluate each case on an individual basis.

So, I was not happy about Gucci going off to the RSPCA. Mmmm, I wonder, my mind started to work overtime. I had an idea that I thought was worth a shot; I wasn't quite sure how I was going to play it, but 'nothing ventured, nothing gained' as they say.
Ring-ring, ring-ring.

"Hi babe, how's the move going?" Ronnie answered

"Oh, you know, hard work, but we're getting there. We're just started to pack the cars for the first trip."

"So what time do you think you'll be finished?"

"It will probably take at least two or three hours, we'll have to make at least three trips, and then there'll be the obligatory pub break of course."

"Well don't strain anything; you know you're not used to physical work." (This was very true. The only exercise I did at that time was lifting my pint of Guinness).

"OK, I'll do my best. Oh, by the way, do you like cats?" (Despite being married nearly two years, and both of us being mad animal lovers, for some reason this subject had never come up).

"Why?"

"Oh, just asking. You're not allergic to them, are you?"

"No, I'm not. Why?"

"Just curious. How do you think Tim feels about cats?"

"I don't know." *Short pause.* "What have you done?" (She knew me far too well, and by this point, she was getting extremely suspicious that I had done something impetuous.)

Time to come clean, so I told her the sorry tale about Gucci, and this time I told it as it was, with no storytelling.

"So, what do you think? Do you think she could come and live with us?"

"Oh." *A bit of a longer pause.* "Well only on the condition that Tim gets on with her." (Truth be told, she is as big a sucker when it comes to animals like me, and just cannot say no to an animal in distress).

And that was how Gucci came to join the ever-growing family. As it turned out, Tim didn't seem to mind Gucci at all. Gucci soon learned that Tim didn't move very fast due to his arthritis, so she had nothing to worry about either. Tim was very good with all the animals in the house, as he just did not seem to care one way or the other. Once, when Ronnie was giving Wayne his monthly brush, he jumped off her lap and ran across Tim's nose. Tim just looked up, stared at Wayne, and then went back to sleep. Gucci, on the other hand, had a lot of devilment in her and was forever teasing Tim. I remember her once sitting on top of the coffee table in the lounge, with Tim in his usual position, asleep half underneath with just his head poking out. She raised a paw, seemed to think about something, and then whacked him on the top of the head. He leapt up looking around for something, or someone to nip. Gucci just continued to sit on the table looking as if she was laughing like a drain. Cats can be very cruel sometimes, but they can also be very funny.

Apart from the nipping, Tim only had one other fault; he took an intense dislike to a wooden rabbit that we had. One year I was really struggling to find a present for Ronnie, and I happened to be in town when I saw this wooden rabbit in the window of a shop. With her predilection for rodents, I thought that this would make an excellent present. So in I went and bought it. It was not cheap, priced at thirty-six pounds, but it was so beautifully carved that I was sure she would love it. I was right, she thought it was brilliant, and promptly named it Joey; I think this might have been after the character from Friends. The problem was that Tim loved it as well, but not in a nice way. I came home from work one day to find that Tim had chewed the ears off Joey. Maybe he simply took a dislike to him, or it might have been that Joey was a better poker player than him, and after losing a whole week's supply of Bonios, Tim took it out of his ears.

What to do? Ronnie had not yet become used to the peculiarities of owning a dog, and I thought that she might be a bit upset. So I decided to go straight into town and buy a replacement. Thirty-six pounds and half an hour later, 'Joey' was back in his rightful place on the floor in the lounge. I didn't even think twice about this, as in the year that we had had Tim, he had never chewed anything before. You can imagine my disbelief, when arriving back from work one day the following week, to find that he had had another go at Joey. This time, he had chewed not only the ears but the legs as well. It looked like another poker session had not gone well for Tim. Well, there was nothing for it, I had to make another trip back to town and spend another thirty-six pounds, Joey was proving to be one of the most expensive presents ever. When I arrived home from work a couple of days later and found that Tim had done it again, I gave up and told Ronnie. As it turned out, she was most understanding, and we both went back to town to get another one, but this time we put 'Joey' on a shelf out of Tim's reach. I think they still play poker together, but either Tim has got better, or maybe one of the rodents adjudicates, either way, Joey was never chewed again.

Well, we had Tim for four years overall, until he finally gave up the ghost and passed away peacefully in his sleep. He managed to reach the grand old age of fifteen, which is pretty good going. By this time, though, he was suffering from arthritis in a bad way and was having trouble getting down, as well as up. If it were not for the fact that he still seemed to enjoy life so much, we might well have had to make that difficult choice that no dog owner likes to make. I really don't know whether it was better or not, but Tim passed away while we were on holiday in Turkey. Two days before we were due to come home, I received a phone call from the Kennels with the bad news. We were both distraught, and feeling just a bit guilty. One small consolation was that the place we were staying had three cats and a dog that belonged to the owners. We spent those last two days giving a lot of attention to those animals, and in their own way, they helped us deal with the immediate grief. The owners, animal lovers both, sat with us well into the night drinking and sharing stories about our animals. Would we have rather been there when he passed away? I don't know, to be honest. In some ways, it would have been better, but in others, it would have been a lot harder.

We considered ourselves very lucky to have had Tim to share our lives. He may have been the grouchiest dog in the world, but he was such a character and gave so much back, he was impossible not to love. Ronnie had by then become a true dog, person. She had really taken Tim into her heart, and she was as devastated as I was when he left us. We decided not to get another dog at that time; it just didn't seem right somehow. This seems to be the same with most animal lovers, I know it doesn't make sense, but that seems to be the way it is. However, we could not keep from missing that love that a dog gives. Both Ronnie and I were miserable, there were so many things in the house, and in our routine, that kept reminding us of Tim. Every night as we were going to bed we would automatically check the space at the bottom of the stairs where Tim used to sleep, half expecting to see him there looking back up at us. We managed to last a whole month before one of us was brave enough to bring up the subject of getting another dog. We felt as though we were being a bit unfaithful to Tim, but something was missing in our lives, and that something was a dog. We just had to start looking for another chap to share it with us.

Tim in his favourite spot (aged 13 years)

Chapter 2 - The puppy arrives

There be trials and tribulations of being a parent to a puppy. If they were not so cute, would we still do it?

Ronnie had decided she wanted a Northern type dog, a Husky or Malamute, or something along similar lines. The first places we looked were the local dog rescue centres, including the Blue Cross in Felixstowe. Though of course, we were very careful to avoid the manageress. However, as they had no dogs available that fit the bill, we started keeping our eyes open for anywhere there might be an advertisement. For the next two weeks, we searched the local papers, eagerly reading the 'Dogs for Sale' section, and looking in every window that had those 'for sale' postcards in them. One day we were at a local pet supplies store, not Pets at Home for a change.

We had gone there to pick up some bedding for the rodents. Ronnie would only buy a certain type of hay, called Meadow Hay, as she was convinced that the rodents preferred this to any other. As this hay was no longer available at Pets at Home, we had to travel to just outside town to another pet store to get it. While at the counter waiting to pay, we idly scanned the adverts for puppies for sale. There were plenty there, but they seemed to be the usual assortment of spaniels, Labradors, and so on. There was one that caught my eye, so after paying, we went over to the board and had a closer look at it.

"Now there's an interesting mix," I said, reading the advertisement. "Irish Wolfhound crossed with Rottweiler. And look, they're only fifty quid. I'd just love to see what they turn out like". I turned around and looked at Ronnie. But judging by the sheer look of terror on her face, it looked like this one was a no. A shame I thought, as they would be a very interesting, more of a donkey than a dog, but all the same, I would have loved to see them.

"What about this one?" asked Ronnie.

Tucked into the corner of the board was an advert for British-Inuit puppies. There was a description stating they were a 'wolfy' type of dog. I had never heard of the British-Inuit breed, but I assumed they were some sort of Northern dog. I knew from experience that most Northern type dogs could be quite independent and stubborn, but at the same time pretty smart, so I thought that this could be interesting.

"I've never heard of them. Tell you what, let's go home, and do a bit of digging on the web," I suggested.

The asking price was five hundred pounds, which I thought reasonable for a 'pedigree' dog. Little did we know at that time, the true cost of what this little puppy would cost us, and that the initial five hundred pounds was to be but a drop in the ocean. We hurriedly took down the breeder's details, sped back home and logged onto the Internet. After a bit of Googling, we came across the British-Inuit Dog Club website, and I'm afraid that was that what fantastic looking dogs. Apparently, the breed was started about 20 years ago and was a mix of Malamute, Husky, German Shepherd, and Czech Wolf dog.

"That's quite a mixture" I mused, "although the German Shepherd should add a bit of trainability."

"But they look so gorgeous."

"They certainly do. What does it say about the Czech Wolfdog mix? "

I will admit I was a little concerned, the German Shepherd being renowned for their "territorialness," and being one-man dogs, might not be ideal with Ronnie's lack of experience. While I was happy and confident with any breed, I wanted to make sure that whatever dog we finally decided upon, was not going to be a problem for Ronnie.

Some Northern type dogs are well known for their strong territorial traits, as well as being a bit crazy, which could be an issue.

"It says the Czech Wolfdog was added to make them easier to train," she had read further on. Then we read a bit further and reached a bit that said, 'if you want a guard dog, do not get a British-Inuit.' This reassured me somewhat as it implied that the breed was not too possessive or protective.

The list of the breed's characteristics looked very promising, 'lively, active, resistant to weather conditions, versatile, friendly and non-guarding.' We found another website for British Inuits, and this was filled with even more comprehensive information on the breed. The site had a quote that also looked promising; 'These beautiful dogs make wonderful family pets, are easily trained, and are good with children and get on well with other pets.'

The ability to get on with other pets was an essential characteristic of whatever type of dog we ended up getting. We wanted to make sure that the new dog would get along with Gucci, and the rodents. "Let's phone, let's phone, please" whimpered Ronnie, so I telephoned the breeders. Yes, they had three dogs left, two boys and a girl, and yes, we could go and visit that afternoon. A happy expectation filled those next two hours, could we have finally found our newest family member.

What a wonderful bundle of pups, a few had been bought but not yet picked up, so there was quite a number tumbling around. Ronnie said it was between the boys, but she just couldn't make her mind up between the two of them. I must admit I was glad to hear this, as I had always had boys and was not sure whether I really wanted a girl. The pups were all fairly lively and running around bouncing off each other like furry pinballs. The parents were two beautiful dogs, the mother had light coloured markings with a slightly long coat, and the father had a shorter coat, but he had some very striking markings. Both of the parents had what seemed very good temperaments, this was very important to us, for as much as we loved Tim we didn't want another dog that was quite as grouchy.

Of the two available boys, the breeder said the red coloured one was the quieter of the two (for 'quieter' I should have translated this to mean simpler). This was what made our minds up. I thought he was, in all likelihood, going to end up a crazy nut case anyway. All my previous dogs had been a little mental, so if he was quiet to start with we may stand a better chance of a 'normal' dog. The choice was made, and he we decided he was the one that we wanted. Our lives were about to change in a most dramatic way.

Our boy aged three months, irresistible

We decided to take him home with us that very afternoon, and so after going through his documentation, and making sure his medicals were all OK, we handed over the pounds and took possession of this wonderful cute fluffy bundle. After a tearful farewell from the breeder, we got into the car with him. I drove, and Ronnie sat in the back, with him sprawled across her lap, he was a fair-sized puppy even at 15 weeks. He had huge paws, enormous pointy ears, and the longest tongue I had ever seen on a dog. It looked as though it should have belonged to a donkey, it must have measured almost a foot. That tongue really was quite amazing. It seemed to loll out like a cartoon character, and by the time we arrived home, he could have filled a family sized bucket from KFC with all the dripping from it. Luckily, the breeder already had him used to travelling in a car, so during the drive home, he was fairly calm, and we thankfully didn't have any accidents.

It took us about half an hour to drive home, and on the way Ronnie pointed out all the green spaces to the dog, telling him that this was where we were going to take him for walks. I, on the other hand, kept my eyes open for any nearby pubs that we could retire to after the said walks. It looked as though I was going to have to get used to doing some exercise. And, if that was the case, then I wanted to make sure that I was going to get some reward for it. A couple of nice pints of Guinness would do the trick.

When we arrived home, we carried the dog into the house through the front door. We then let him down onto the hall floor and walked slowly with him towards the lounge, both of us making encouraging noises along the way. He was very tentative, not nervous exactly, but as if he was not sure of his new surroundings, you could tell he wanted to make sure that he wasn't walking into trouble. Slowly he walked down the hall, and then came to the kitchen doorway, but at this point, he stopped, he was not happy. He kept peering around the doorjamb as though he expected a big monster to jump out and attack him.

After a fair amount of encouragement, he eventually made it through to the lounge. We sat down on the sofa and Ronnie started to call him up to sit beside her, I must admit I was not too sure about letting him on the sofa. My reasoning for this was, that if we started letting him on from the start, then we were going to have trouble stopping him when he started getting bigger. Moreover, there was no doubt looking at those huge paws of his, that he was going to grow into a fair-sized dog. She won that argument. She was so happy with her new dog. So much so that she wasn't going to miss out on the chance of giving him lots of cuddles, and for her, the sofa was the best place to do this. He still gets on the sofa to this day, but he does it in a kind of stealth mode. First, he places one paw on my lap, then another, and then he slides forward until his stomach is resting on my legs. He then does what I can only describe as a spinning motion, where all of him ends up on the sofa, and me, but upside down. He will lie there contentedly while receiving lots of attention, and after ten minutes, he will slide off.

As we sat on the sofa, with the fella sprawling across Ronnie's lap, we started discussing names for him. His kennel name was Lakota, but we didn't fancy calling him that that, we wanted to give him a name of our own choosing, and something a bit more personal to us.

"How about John or Robert?" I suggested

"I don't think your dad or brother would be very pleased with you naming a dog after them."

We lazed around for the next couple of hours and had a few drinks, a few beers for me, and a couple of glasses of wine for Ronnie. We discussed plenty of different names for him, and had a few hours of laughter until I finally said: "How about Kopek?"

Now you may or may not know, but a Kopek was a small coin of Russian origin, but it is also the Turkish word for dog. We both love Turkey and have had many a happy holiday there. It also somehow seemed fitting, as that was where we were when we lost Tim. Plus we thought, in our slightly befuddled alcoholic state, it would be quite amusing. So the decision was made, and he was called Kopek. On occasion, while we have been out walking with Kopek, someone has stopped us in the street and asked his name. We both find it amusing to watch that look of confusion cross their face, as they tried to figure out why on Earth anyone would call their dog after a small Russian coin. We cannot wait until we meet someone from Turkey, can you imagine the conversation in Turkish.

"What's your dog called?"

"Dog."

"Yes, but what's his name?"

We had decided from the start that the kitchen was the best place to feed Kopek because apart from the lounge, this was the only room on the ground floor that did not have a carpet. This turned out to be a very wise decision, as Kopek is the sloppiest drinker I have ever known, and I include myself after ten pints in this comparison. I'm sure it is because of that enormous tongue of his; he leaves so much water on the floor; it's as though he can't control. After he had finished his dinner, which he wolfed down like a starving piranha, we let him out into the back garden. At first, he wouldn't even step out of the kitchen door, but with plenty of encouragement, he finally made those first few brave steps. When he got to the lawn, his demeanour changed, he seemed to love it, and he started sniffing and walking around without needing any further cajoling.

As by then, we had accumulated three rabbits and a guinea pig, I had built a twelve-foot by five-foot run for them. This sat alongside the fence running down our back garden. The run was constructed out of long lengths of timber and had chicken wire fixed all around the sides. It even had three separate tops for it, again with wire coverings, so there was plenty of room to house their two hutches inside. This was a mammoth task for me to build because; a) I'm not very good when it comes to working with wood, and b) it was quite hard physical work. Despite my natural aversion to any type of physical labour, I'm pretty good with tools. I have managed to finish some fairly major projects in my time, but the one thing I have never had an aptitude with was wood. This meant that it took me a good two weeks to complete the rabbit run, and it cost me several pounds more than it should have due to me miss-measuring the wood. Once finished, though, it was a masterpiece, at least by my standards of woodworking. It meant that we could let the rodents out every morning, and they had as much grass as they wanted. Every night we would put them away, back into their hutches.

Little did we know it then, but within the next couple of months, we were to lose two of the rabbits. One night some animal managed to get into the run, and in the morning I found Ali dead. She had been viciously attacked, and Steve was nowhere to be seen. We did find him later that morning, in the small gap between the back of the garage and the neighbour's fence. There was not a scratch on him, so we suspect he must have simply died of fright. Oddly enough, both

Donald and Wayne were still alive, but when I looked, there was no doubt a fox had found its way into the run. There were the unmistakable paw prints of a fox in the soil and signs of a big disturbance in one corner where there had obviously been a fight of some kind. We puzzled over this for the rest of the day, how had Donald and Wayne survived? It is very unusual for anything to survive a fox attack, as they normally go into a killing frenzy. It was not until the next day that we noticed that Donald was lame in one of his back legs. When we took him to the vets, they said that is was likely that he had kicked the fox so hard he had broken his foot. Thankfully, Donald made a full recovery within a week or so. I tell you, he was one mean tough rabbit.

During Kopek's mooching around the garden, he came across the rodent run. He sniffed his way around and then came face to face with Donald on the other side of the wire. Now as I have mentioned, Donald was a tough old rabbit, and he wasn't afraid of anything, let alone some nervous bundle of fur. He simply stood his ground and stared at Kopek, they were almost nose-to-nose through the wire. Suddenly Donald sneezed, and Kopek took an almighty leap backwards. I had never seen a dog jump backwards before, and it was quite a funny sight. He then did the dog dance thing, the one when they stick their bum in the air and bounce on their front feet while at the same time keeping their back feet almost nailed to one spot. Donald just looked on in a disdainful manner. It was as though he was saying, "What a muppet, you'd never catch a self-respecting rabbit doing that sort of thing."

After that first encounter, Kopek never did bother the rodents, but he always kept a keen interest in them. Quite often, we would see him in the back garden lying down next to the run, with his nose about two inches away from the wire. He seemed quite happy to spend ages simply watching them going about their business of eating the grass. Kopek was not the only one who found the rodents fascinating, as we often saw Gucci either asleep or just resting on top of their run. I never once saw her do any more than watch them, but that's not to say she wouldn't have if she got the chance. The rodents soon became used to being watched, and they tended to just ignore both of them. Ronnie suggested that they thought it was some form of rodent Big Brother.

"Please report to the hutch, Donald. What do you think of the little furry one above your run?"

"I think she's a sneaky one that, she pretends not to watch, but I've seen her looking at my carrots out the corner of her eye."

"Have you anything else to say?"

"Yes, when are you going to evict that smelly guinea pig?"

"Being smelly isn't a good enough reason to be evicted."

"But he keeps me awake at night with his snoring, and then there are his all-night poker sessions. I'm surprised he hasn't set alight to the hutch the amount he smokes."

"Please report to the hutch, Wayne. Have you any requests?"

"Yes, when are you going to evict that smelly rabbit...."

That first evening we played with Kopek for a little while, and then he would flop over Ronnie's lap while we watched television. I was still not happy about allowing Kopek on the sofa, but she was having none of it. She loved having him draped over her lap, like an oversized napkin. Despite my protestations, I still didn't think it had quite sunk in yet with Ronnie, just how big Kopek was going to grow. If his paws and ears were anything to go by he was going to be quite a big fella indeed, and God help us if he ever grew into that tongue, he would be the size of a cow.

As evening drew on, and it was well past the watershed, we thought we would head for bed. Now I'm sure any of you who have owned a puppy will know this is a difficult time for all, puppies, and humans. We had decided that we would be strict, and make Kopek sleep in the kitchen during the night. Under no circumstances were we going to allow him upstairs in the bedroom with us, at least not during the night. This hadn't been a problem with Tim, due to his arthritis. Tim wasn't too keen on going upstairs anyway, as that generally meant he was going to have his monthly bath, and he didn't like that one bit. We had done the obvious things in the kitchen in readiness for Kopek. We had cleared the floor, laid down loads of newspaper, and fluffed up his new bed. We had also bought him a new toy, which we were letting him keep throughout the night. I had gone and bought an old-style alarm clock, one of those that make a loud tick-tock, and we wrapped that up in a blanket in his bed. There is a theory that puppies think that this is their mother's heartbeat, it helps them settle in the night, and I was hoping this would work.

It was difficult to leave him there on his own, his big brown puppy eyes staring at us, his daft tongue hanging out the side of his mouth. It was almost as if he was saying, "Don't leave me. There's still a load of time to play yet." Nevertheless, we could delay no longer, we went upstairs to bed, and then it started. At first, it was just a few yelps and whines, but it then built up to a full-scale howl. This would go on for a solid hour, followed by about ten minutes of peace where we thought he had settled down. But no, off he would start, howling again. We were both astonished at the volume from such a small puppy, he really did sound like a wolf. This carried on all through the night and into the early hours, right up until we got up in the morning. On arising, none of us had had much sleep, Ronnie, Kopek, or me, but we decided we should keep at it. That is Ronnie, and I decided, I don't think that Kopek was too keen on the idea. "It may be pitiful, but we need to keep persevering," I said to Ronnie. "If we give in, he'll have us wrapped around his little claw, and we'll never get him to stay on his own. We have to show him who's the boss." I was determined that Kopek was not going to grow up thinking he was the alpha dog in our family pack. This was the problem we had had with Tim, and we never did manage to completely cure him of it. I did not want the same thing happening with Kopek; he would make our lives hell if he thought he was top dog.

The next day was even better. As Kopek became a bit more confident, he started to play, grabbing hold of my arm, or trouser leg, and ragging it. He loved to hook his legs around my ankles, then grab hold of my jeans with his teeth, and shake his head vigorously from side to side. I had forgotten just how sharp puppy teeth could be, and I lost a fair bit of skin and blood while playing with him. It became very clear, right from the start that Kopek simply loved to shred things. Anything he found that would fit into his mouth he would chew. I'd found an old tennis ball that I would roll down the lounge, and he would scamper after it, his tail wagging furiously. I would then spend the next five minutes trying to get it back off him. After half an hour, we were both in need of a breather from the playing, at least I was, I think Kopek was still up for more. I was knackered; this was more exercise that I had done in years. So I left him alone with the tennis ball, and when I checked on him ten minutes later, it was completely bald. He had, quiet as a mouse, plucked all the fur off with his front teeth. A further five minutes, and the tennis ball was no more, it was in lots of tiny pieces spread all around him.

This was the day that Kopek had his first visit to the vets. We both bundled him into the car, and headed off to the clinic, as we use the same vets for all our animals. Our appointment was for two-thirty, and we arrived in plenty of time with about fifteen minutes to spare. I was particularly happy at being early, as this gave me a perfect opportunity for a bit of animal indulgence. It was amusing to watch the indecision in Kopek, he was quite nervous about being in a strange place, but on the other hand, there were so many tantalising new smells. We had only been sitting there for five minutes when in came an old woman with a young Boxer dog. He can't have been more than five, or six months old, and the little mite had a tea towel wrapped around one of his feet.

"Poor fella. What happened to him?" I asked her.

"He hurt his leg on some broken glass, playing on the field I take him for walks on. Bloody kids, why they can't clear up after themselves is beyond me."

Being a bit of a grouch myself when it comes to kids, I felt myself warming to this old dear. With desperation, she was straining to hold onto the lead, trying to keep him away from Kopek, who at that moment was hiding behind Ronnie. Without warning, Kopek shot out, and with one of his paws gave the Boxer a playful whack on the nose. The Boxer, despite his injury, was all up for a play. From that point, all hell broke loose, as the two of them started running around. The ever-shortening leads were drawing Ronnie and the woman inevitably closer together. A Pointer, which had been sitting quietly in the corner, then tried to join in, and a Scottie on the other side of the waiting room set off barking. There was a massive tangle of leads and owners, as we tried to sort ourselves, and our dogs out. At one point, I ended up on the floor with an armful of dog, I'm not sure which one, but grabbing any of them would have helped at that point.

We eventually sorted ourselves out, with no help from the dogs, I might add, and it was that point that I noticed I had a rather wet leg. One of them, I had no idea which one had felt the need to relieve themselves during the struggle, and had thought my leg was the best place to do it. I sat myself down, praying that it wouldn't be too long before the vet called us; Kopek had not made a very good first impression. For the next ten minutes, every dog that came into the clinic was met with lunges from all corners of the room, along with a cacophony of whines, barks, and howls.

Finally, the vet called us in, and I dragged Kopek along. Thankfully, they have a nice smooth floor, as Kopek had decided he had had enough and was sitting down. He may well have received some burn marks on his backside; such was the speed I pulled him into the examination room. I wasn't going to give him the opportunity to cause any more havoc.

The vet had just closed the door when I said "Sorry."

"What for?" He asked

"That," I said, pointing at the floor.

"What? Oh, I see. Don't worry about it, many dogs defecate in here. I just hope it's not personal." He said with a smile. "Is he friendly?"

"Soft as anything, and daft as a brush," I assured him.

There was a feeling of relief as the examination went smoothly, and Kopek passed with flying colours. He didn't even flinch when the vet gave him his jabs, he really could be a good boy, sometimes. I always have that little nagging feeling when I take a new dog for their first visit to the vets. I suppose I'm afraid that there might be something seriously wrong with them.

When we arrived back home, I announced to Ronnie that I was off to Pets at Home to get him some proper toys. I was going to become even more familiar with this place in the next few months. Half an hour later, I arrived back home with an armful of toys and chews.

"That's enough to last him a month," Ronnie pointed out

"Well I couldn't decide which toy to buy; there was just so much good stuff," I responded. "Anyhow, you should be thankful I didn't come back with another furry."

"True I suppose," sighed Ronnie.

This was when we realised that Kopek could chew, and I mean really chew. He went through one of those rawhide bones in about five minutes flat. I know it was only a small six-inch one, but even so, he was only four months old. I tried him with one of those rubber rings, the ones that you can play tug-of-war with. He loved it, and we tugged each other around the lounge for about half an hour, after which I needed another breather. I realised then that I was going to have to get a little fitter if I was going to have enough energy to play with Kopek. When I checked back on him 10 minutes later, the ring was in four pieces. I still have no idea how he did it so quickly, or so quietly.

According to the breeder, they had partially housetrained Kopek. We soon found out what 'partially' meant, and he had several small accidents during the day. It was only his peeing that we needed to address, for the other he would walk in circles and whine a little. However, he didn't seem to understand that he also needed to do this when he wanted to pee. I think that this is probably the most stressful part of owning a young dog. All we could do was to try to get Kopek to understand he needed to tell us, whenever he felt the need to pee.

In most cases, housetraining takes time, often lots and lots of time, but we were quite lucky with Kopek. He picked up pretty quickly that he must not do his stuff in the house, or at least anywhere but on what was left of the paper. It was not long before we could reduce the amount of newspaper that we had to lay down, to a small area of about three pages of a broadsheet. The trouble was, it took quite a long time to get to the next stage of getting him to go outside. I think part of the problem was that he enjoyed shredding the paper so much, there was often nothing left for him to go on. By late afternoon my patience had worn thin, I had replaced the newspaper about four times by then. I decided to get some of those special dog pads, off to Pets at Home, yet again. These were chemically treated pads to make them irresistible to dogs. This was supposed to ensure that they would do their business on them. While Kopek certainly found them irresistible; it was not in the way the manufacturer had intended. He enjoyed shredding these even more than he enjoyed shredding the newspaper. As we were not made of money, and the pads were not cheap, we decided we would return to using the newspaper and just persevere.

Previously, days spent at home followed a similar pattern, we would watch a bit of television, do a bit of surfing on the Internet and read for a bit. This is how the day went for us now, except that these things were now interspersed with playing with Kopek. Most weeks, we went to the pub two or three times, but as Kopek had only just had his jabs, we couldn't take him out for a whole week. As we didn't want to leave him on his own yet, we stayed in, amused ourselves and played with him. I cannot even begin to tell you how much of a sacrifice this was, no Guinness for a week. The things we do for our dogs eh?

Early on the second evening, we were very tired, mainly due to the lack of sleep from the night before, so we headed to bed a little earlier than normal.

"OK fella, it's time for bed now." How is it that a dog can make you feel so guilty with just a look?

"Would it be so bad if we let him come upstairs with us?" Ronnie asked. "Look at those puppy eyes."

"C'mon, we must be strong. We can't let him know he can get one over on us by howling. If he realises that by howling he can get his own way, he'll never stop."

"I suppose you're right. It's just so heartrending."

"It's very important to make him understand that he is not the boss." I was being strong for the both of us.

The howls started before we could make it to the top of the stairs, and boy could he howl. It was pitiful, and yes, it went on all night, only stopping completely when we got up in the morning. To give you an idea just how loud the howling was, the next day our neighbour called. She is a very nice lady and not one to normally complain. However, this morning, she knocked on the door and asked if we wouldn't mind leaving Kopek in the kitchen at night. Her son's bedroom backed onto our party wall; she explained, and the howling was keeping him awake. Understandably, she was surprised when we told her that we already left him in the kitchen during the night, as this is on the opposite side of the house. I apologised profusely and explained that we hoped it would subside in a couple more days at most. Unfortunately, this turned out to be the height of optimism. It was exactly the same the next night, and the next, and the next, and after five nights, we caved. It didn't matter what we tried, and, believe me, we tried all sorts, he simply howled the whole night through. We were both absolutely shattered, as neither of us had had any sleep for a week. Kopek was not in much better shape, although he managed to catch up during the day.

We were determined not to completely admit defeat with the discipline, so we moved his bed upstairs to our bedroom and put it at the bottom of our bed. We were not going to give him an outright victory and allow him on our bed. I may have lost the sofa argument, but there was no way I was going to share the bed with a dog that was going to be the size Kopek was growing into. However, he was content with just being in the same room as us. It was like having a different dog, and he simply curled up and went to sleep. From that point on, he slept with us in our bedroom, and he then thought he knew exactly who the boss was. He may have won the battle, but the war was far from over!

Chapter 3 - The first few months

*Surely, it cannot just be me. Why do dogs
like to eat everything they shouldn't?*

We had both taken a bit of time off work for this first week, as we had thought it was best if we could spend as much time with him as possible as he became used to his new surroundings. Unfortunately, it was now time to go back to work. I'm lucky in that I work in an IT department, and this means that I can work from home quite a lot, or if I am unable to work from home, I can at least go in late or come home early most days. Also, I only live five minutes from work, so I'm able to pop back home easily if I have to do a whole day out of the house. This meant that I could check up on how Kopek was getting on in between my meetings. Ronnie is also able to work from home a couple of days a week most of the time, so between us we thought it would be a rare occasion that Kopek was going to be on his own for more than two or three hours. During the previous week, we had tried leaving him on his own in the kitchen for five minutes, then ten minutes, and finally had it to half an hour. We had once even managed an hour on his own while we sat in the lounge with a mug of coffee and a couple of books while listening out for any signs of his distress. There was a fair bit of snuffling around, and a couple of minutes or so of some sad howling, but overall, he seemed to cope with it OK.

Although the session he was on his own for an hour, he did manage to eat a brush and make a start on a mop. This was probably the reason why there was so little howling. There was also the obligatory shredding of the newspaper, and then peeing where the newspaper used to be. I think he thought we left it for him to either eat or entertain himself. I am sure this is where he started to get his taste for paper. He had started to shred anything made of paper that he came across in the house; that is when no one was looking. Whenever he was on his own, and he came across paper, he set off stripping it into very small wet bits. As Kopek hadn't seemed to mind being on his own too much, we were optimistic that he would be fine on the odd occasion that we both had to be out at work at the same time.

My first day back at work, and I had a meeting at ten o'clock. Unfortunately, I couldn't attend the meeting over a conference call, so I had to go into the office. I had left Kopek in the kitchen with a small amount of food, a full water bowl, and a couple of his toys. The meeting, scheduled for an hour and a half, meant that Kopek would be on his own for around two hours. I had hoped it wouldn't drag on, as. I didn't want to leave it much longer than that before I could check back on Kopek and see how he was coping. But as is often the case, there was a person there who insisted on using twenty words when one or two would have been more than ample, and the meeting went on for an extra thirty minutes before I managed to get away.

I drove up to the house, and on getting out of the car, I thought "Not too bad, at least there was no howling." I opened the front door, went in, and tentatively opened the kitchen door. A mass of fur, paws and an enormous tongue promptly bowled me over. Even at four months, Kopek was quite a powerful dog. In the kitchen, there was not much left of the newspaper we had left down, at least nothing that could have been identified as a newspaper. He had left me a present to clean up, right where the paper should have been. Ah, my shoes, I had forgotten to move them out of the kitchen. They were a pair of hideous slip-ons made of suede. One day for some reason, I had thought, "I'd like a pair of those." I had bought them on eBay, and when they arrived, Ronnie was less than impressed.

"What on Earth possessed you to buy those?" She asked, with a look on her face that was akin to if she had just discovered a snail in her boiled egg. "They look like a pair of shoes that your grand-dad would buy."

To tell the truth, despite my trying to argue in favour of them, I was not overly impressed with them either. This is the other side of my impulsiveness. Once I get an idea to buy something, I don't often take the time to think it through, I just go ahead and buy whatever object has taken my fancy. Our house is full of 'stuff' I have bought off eBay. I wouldn't go as far as to say I'm an addict, but there are just so many things on the auction site, that look like a great idea at the time. Moreover, if I say so myself, I am rather good at the bidding thing. Although, as Ronnie likes to point out, I'm not very good at the getting rid of them thing. Oh well, as I had said, I didn't much care for the shoes anyway. They weren't completely destroyed, Kopek had simply removed the soles, shredded them, and he had then chewed the edges a bit, just enough to give them that jagged look. "I suppose they will keep for trekking out to the garden to feed the rodents in the mornings." I thought to myself.

I spent the next ten minutes calming Kopek down and then put him outside in the back garden while I set about cleaning up the kitchen. Once it was sparkly clean (Ronnie's normal standard), I let him back in and went into the front room. I set up my laptop so I could carry on working from home for the rest of the day. The front room of the house has always been my domain, and Ronnie refuses even to go in there to clean. This was my playroom, and the only time she reluctantly enters is to hunt for a missing plate or mug. This would be one I had taken in at some point during the day but hadn't yet returned to the kitchen. My room is where I keep my guitars, music paraphernalia, and often the final resting place for the 'stuff' I have bought off eBay. It's also where my desk and the computer is set up; it is a real boy's room. The majority of our male friends are most envious of it, and I think truth be told, their other halves are as well.

When I looked over, Kopek appeared blissfully happy, curled up asleep by the door. Kopek was starting to develop two modes. The first was almost lethargic, in that he would happily lie around for a couple of hours, either asleep or simply watching the world go by. The second mode, however, was full-scale hyperactive. For instance, when I picked up one of his toys to play, he would go into a whirlwind of manic energy, jumping up and ragging the toy, my arms, and my legs. What was somewhat disconcerting is that he could move from one mode to the other in a blink of an eye. Dare to pick up a toy, and he would go from lethargic sprawl to tugging your arm off within seconds, there didn't seem to be anything in the middle.

Kopek aged four months

Why is it that a dog can always find something to destroy, even in what you think is a completely cleared room? When we had decided to leave Kopek in the kitchen, we had expected him to have a go at the cupboards. As I mentioned earlier, the kitchen was one of the rooms where we had not spent much time renovating, with its old worktop and very tired cupboards. We had planned to update it sometime soon but thought it would be more sensible to wait, at least until Kopek had gone through the chewing stage that every puppy seems to go through. Not once did he eat any part of that kitchen, not the tatty doors, or the old bits of edging that never seem quite to reach the floor. He did, however, help himself to anything and everything that was not nailed down, or hidden away in a cupboard, which thankfully, he never did learn to open.

For those next few weeks, we would leave Kopek alone for an hour, or at most, two hours at a time. We were deliberately trying to build up the time because very occasionally he was going to have to do up to a four-hour stint. Even when I was working from home, I would put him in the kitchen for a time, just to try to get him used to it. Every time he was left, there was something else gone. A mop, brush, the plastic thing that you put your knives and forks into dry, another mop, and one time half a dozen eggs that we had forgotten to put away. That I can tell you was not a very pleasant experience when it eventually made a re-appearance. If I were working from home, and hear a crash, I would go running into the kitchen. I would open the door, to find him ragging some object or other. He would then look up at me as if to say "What? Didn't you leave this for me to play with?"

I must admit, I was getting a little concerned at the state Kopek was getting himself into when we left him in the kitchen, he really did not like being in there on his own. When I opened the door to free him, he would go crazy for about five minutes, tearing around the house, or the back garden, it put me in mind of a ferret that had recently eaten a Vindaloo. It was time to have another chat with Ronnie.

"Maybe he's just bored," I suggested. "Perhaps if he's a bit more room he wouldn't feel so penned in, and would calm down a bit."

"Well, there's no way he's having the run of the house," Ronnie stated, quite categorically. She had seen the remains of the mops and brushes and had no intention of giving him the chance to do this to the rest of the house.

"What about, if we somehow barricaded the lounge and the stairs off? That should limit the space and potential for destruction a bit. We have to do something, he really isn't happy in the kitchen."

"C'mon, I have an idea," said Ronnie.

We put Kopek in the back of the car, and Ronnie drove us to Pets at Home. I had hoped to go a whole week without having to go there, my limit being three days so far. Ronnie pointed over to some cardboard boxes stacked up in one corner.

"You're a genius," I declared.

Having invested in two large sized dog gates, we set off back home. Despite us only being in the shop for fifteen minutes, Kopek had managed to fill this time by chewing the handbrake. Here's a hint for all you soon to be parents out here, dog gates are cheaper than baby gates, and as far as I can tell, they're exactly the same.

Our lounge has no door on it, so that was where gate number one went. Gate number two went on the first step of the stairs and attached to the wall and the banister.

"That should do it," I said to Ronnie in a most confident manner, "there's no way he'll get around those."

"Are you sure they're secure?" She asked. She was well aware of my inadequacies when it came to anything with wood involved.

"Of course," I said, offended that she would doubt me.

"Mmmm, they seem OK." She conceded after giving them a close inspection.

I now felt quite confident that the area he had to roam in was quite secure. Now he had more space; I was sure he wouldn't get quite so worked up. He now had the kitchen and the hall to roam around in, and that was a fair amount of space. Our kitchen is about twenty-five-foot square, and the hall is an 'L' shape, which is about five-foot at its narrowest and is about thirty-five feet long all told. I'm sure those of you still showing the battle scars of recent puppyhood will be smiling knowingly at this point.

I know, I know, I had not fully thought through my plan. While the dog gates might have been a good idea in themselves, the fatal flaw of the plan was that this would now give Kopek a new space in which to find more things to destroy. There was a second flaw in my plan, in that this also gave Kopek the opportunity, should he ever get past the gates, to gain unlimited access to other parts of the house. To begin with, it actually seemed to work, a bit. He certainly wasn't quite as crazed as when he was on his own, but sadly, he didn't stop chewing things. "But hey, one step at a time," I thought, "at least he seems a lot calmer." By the end of the next month, Kopek had very calmly eaten a large chunk of the hall carpet. He had also calmly eaten another course of mop, brush, yet another mop, the doorframes into the kitchen, and for desert, he finished off my suede shoes.

Tasty

The other thing that Kopek now had access to was the front door. The access in itself was not necessarily a problem, it was just that the post arrived through the front door, and that was cause for concern. In some ways, we were lucky that the post normally arrived in the morning, usually around seven thirty, but on the odd occasion, it was as late as ten o'clock. Most of the time, we got to the post before Kopek, but every now and again, when we had both left early for work, and the post was late, he got there first. Whenever this happened, all that remained would be some very small bits of unidentifiable paper strewn over the hall floor, often still wet with dog saliva. A growing theme with Kopek was his absolute love of paper, and he simply thought it the best possible toy in the world. Anytime he was alone, anything made of paper was the first thing to get his attention. His favourite toy at that time was the inside of a toilet roll or kitchen paper roll.

Kopek was getting bigger by the day, which meant that the range of objects within reach of his jaws was growing. He could now reach the kitchen worktops without too much trouble at all, and anything left on there was, as far as he was concerned, left especially for him. It's an odd thing, I can't remember him ever chewing anything left on the kitchen table, but that didn't stop him turning his attention to the table itself and eating the corners off it. It was a gorgeous old pine table; Ronnie's father had made it for her when she first moved out from home. It was a substantial one, with a good three inches of tabletop, big chunky legs, and very nice right-angled corners. Now, there were two chewed rounded ones, as, over the first month he was with us, he had made a concerted effort to nibble a little bit off each corner every day. I can only presume the only reason he didn't chew the other two corners, was that they were against the wall, and that would have been too much of a struggle.

"How do we stop the dog chewing the furniture?" Ronnie asked. She had not been impressed the first time he had done this and was getting less impressed as each day had passed. "If we don't stop him soon they'll be nothing left of it by the end of next month."

"It's difficult," I said. "It's a phase that most dogs go through."

"Well, it'll be a very short phase if he doesn't stop soon because I'll kill him."

Ronnie wasn't in a good mood that day. She had arrived home first, as I had been delayed at work. She had been presented with rather a large amount of wet shredded paper to clean up, as unfortunately, the free paper had arrived while we were out. That, along with yet more of her precious table having disappeared, hadn't put her in the best frame of mind.

It was time to try to put a stop to the chewing of the furniture, before it became a major headache, for both Kopek and me. So yet another visit to Pets at Home ensued. I had seen an advertisement for a spray that was supposed to make things taste nasty to dogs. There were two key words in the advert; the first was 'should,' and the second was 'nasty.' It should have read 'might,' or 'maybe,' or to be more truthful 'probably won't but worth a try.' I suppose I should have thought about this a bit harder, but things are often clearer after the event. It's a sad fact of life that dogs actually like nasty stuff, in fact, the nastier something is, the better, as far as they're concerned. I never found out whether it made things tastier for him or not, but it most certainly didn't seem to deter him at all. Kopek did grow out of the furniture chewing stage quickly, thank goodness, and the phase only seemed to last for about a month longer. And no, before you ask, he still didn't eat any part of the tatty old kitchen cupboards; I think he must have better taste than that.

One of the things that Kopek loves most of all, even more than paper I think, is that first walk in the morning. It was in the first month after he had had his jabs, which he first experienced this. As I have mentioned, we consider ourselves very fortunate living in Suffolk, with its many parks and open spaces. However, even more, fortunate for us is that just down the road, about two hundred yards on the other side is a field that is a haven for dog walkers. The field is about the size of two full sized football pitches, with a small copse, a basketball hoop, and an area with a couple of goalposts. There is also a fenced area with a kiddie's playground in it, with swings, slides, and a climbing frame, this is a no-go area for the dogs.

We had been trying to get Kopek used to the lead over the previous few days, in preparation for his first proper walk. We had been putting it on him and letting him amble around the house, with the lead trailing behind him. We had also used it on him in the back garden, walking him up and down the lawn, and by now, he seemed comfortable with it. On this Saturday, we clipped his lead on and took him out of the house and onto the pavement for the first time. He was not a happy dog, down went his bum, and out went his front legs in that stiff determined way that dogs do. You could see it in his face "whoa, what's this place? I've never seen this before." Well, it took us about half an hour to coax him the two hundred yards to the field, with him sitting down every couple of feet. Ronnie and I had to use all of our persuasive dog skills to encourage him to continue. Once he finally reached the field, he suddenly changed into what seemed a different dog. He was very happy to try to sniff every single blade of grass within the radius of his lead.

Kopek had lost all of his nervousness and was straining at the lead, trying to sniff places that were just out of his reach. After about ten minutes, in which time we had managed to walk a whole five yards, we thought we would try him off the lead, and see how he would take to it. We thought this would be safe enough, as there are only three small entrances to the field, and they all led out onto quiet roads. Even if the worst happened, and he took off out of one, we would be able to catch him easily. Kopek really started to enjoy himself, and he would run off a couple of feet and then run back. He started going in ever-increasing circles, but only going about three or four yards away at the most. Then he saw another dog, and it was like watching a Border Collie on 'One Man and His Dog.' Kopek would take one or two steps, and then sit or lie down. He would then take another couple of steps, and down again. He had got to within about twenty feet of the other dog before he was spotted. The other dog was fairly large, which we since learned was called Missy.

Missy was a cross between a Rottweiler and a Labrador, and she came barrelling over to see Kopek. He was not having any of it, he came tearing back to us with his tail tucked up tight between his legs and kept trying to hide behind us. Missy was about the same age as Kopek but had been going out for a couple of weeks already, so she was a lot more confident than he was. She may have been a big lump, but she was as soft as any dog you could imagine, and all she wanted to do was play. Slowly at first, but growing in confidence with every minute that passed, Kopek started to play with Missy. The fear gradually turned to love, and Kopek became besotted with her over the days that followed. Over the next few days and weeks, Kopek met many other dogs of all shapes and sizes, but I think Missy was always his first love, and anytime she appeared on the field, he would go tearing off towards her. They would then rough and tumble for as long as we would let them, and often longer than we would have liked.

It is an odd thing about dogs, for most of them, every day starts with a walk, and it is the same routine day in day out. Yet they get so excited at the sight of a lead, you would think they had never done it before. Show Kopek his lead, and he went straight into manic mode, racing around and weaving in between our legs. He would then do that little dancing thing, where his front paws lifted about three inches off the floor, in a sort of half jump. All this weaving and dancing, along with those little whining noises he made that sound like a wheelbarrow with a very squeaky wheel. It does make me wonder whether they suffer from some sort of canine Alzheimer's, and they cannot remember that they went for a walk only the day before. Maybe, it's because a dog ages seven years for every one of ours so that for a dog one day equals the same as a week for us.

Kopek's recall was not very good, and that is putting it at its most generous. So Ronnie made the decision that she was going to take him to dog training, classes.

"Good luck," I shouted, as she left for the first lesson. I was not convinced that this was going to have much effect on Kopek.

"At least it should be fun," She called back.

"I'm sure it will be," I sniggered to myself. I had a picture in my mind of a circle of proud owners and their well-behaved dogs, and then Kopek speeding like a deranged dervish among them.

Surprisingly, Kopek took to dog classes as though he was born to it, and after each demonstration of obedience, the teacher was full of praise. Obviously, it took a bit of time for him to understand that the other dogs were not there to play, but after that, he did quite well. The problem was that once Kopek was on the field, he completely forgot everything that he'd learned, and after six lessons, Ronnie stopped going to the classes.

"It's pointless" she explained, "He's one of the best-behaved dogs there. The teacher is always praising him, yet as soon as he's off the lead on the field, poof, it all goes to hell."

To give him his due, though, if there were no other dogs on the field, he was quite obedient. It was only when he was playing that he developed that most common of dog complaints, selective hearing. This was becoming somewhat of a theme with Kopek, as he seemed to be quite a smart dog, in that he would pick up new commands very quickly. Then he seemed to decide whether he was going to obey them, or not, as the case may be. Sometimes you could see him making the decision, he would set off running after another dog, and when I, or

Ronnie, called him back, he would hesitate and slow down slightly. Then his ears would go back, and he would put on an extra spurt of speed. This was the point we knew it was useless to even try to call him back, as he had made his decision. It was as though when he flattened his ears, he was saying "Sorry, I can't hear you."

The local field became a place of absolute joy for Kopek, and it didn't matter where else we would take him, he never got as excited as when he was heading for there. I must admit I loved going there too, as it was a great experience seeing all the other dogs playing together. Along with the usual crowd of morning walkers, of which there were about a dozen dogs, there were always a few new arrivals. These would come and go at intervals during the month. One morning I counted twenty-two dogs running around the field, it was quite an incredible sight. Nevertheless, I would have hated to cross that field if I were not a lover of dogs, as I think it may have been quite intimidating. However, I thought it was brilliant.

Out of the usual crew that visited the field, there was a hard core of dogs, which were firm friends of Kopek. There was Missy, of course, and then there was his other love, Miya. Miya was a beautiful white Alsatian, who was a little bit older than Kopek by a few months, and she owned by my neighbour, Sam, three doors down. Miya lived with Elle, an older Red Setter, who generally plodded around the field, and only occasionally joined in the play. I was always a bit embarrassed when Kopek and Miya played together, as she nearly always ended up filthy, covered in mud and dirt as they tumbled around together. Kopek's favourite trick was to roll the other dogs. As he ran alongside them, he leaned into them at an angle, pushing them with his shoulder, until they tumbled over. As with Missy, if Miya ever appeared on the field, Kopek would stop whatever he was doing and race over to see her. This adoration meant that whenever they were on the field together, that was it, it was then the devil's own job to get them to come back.

Of the other dogs, in the core group of Kopek's friends, there was Oscar, and he was the alpha male of the group. Oscar was as big as Kopek and had some Rottweiler in him somewhere. But he was fairly mild-mannered, apart for the odd occasion when he just set off running and barking into the sky for what seemed like no reason at all, except that he just felt like it. Oscar made sure that all the other dogs behaved themselves. If any of them got a bit too big for their boots, he would mosey on over and assert his dominance.

Then, there were a couple of smaller dogs; there were Scamp and Molly, who were short dark haired terrier types. Molly seemed to love Kopek, and as soon as she saw him, she would rush over and jump up at his face. Scamp would also run over as soon as he saw Kopek, he would then roll over on his back, letting Kopek sniff him all over. Scamp and Molly were only about six or seven inches off the ground, so when they played with Kopek, they had trouble keeping up with his long-legged stride. Mind you, what they lacked in height, they certainly made up for in energy and determination. They both generally ended up very wet after a session with Kopek, either because of Kopek rolling them in the grass or from him play biting them. Scamp in particular always looked the worse for wear because he was longer haired than Molly.

About two or three months after Kopek first discovered the field, Alfred joined us on some of our morning walks. Alfred was one crazy Staffordshire bull terrier, who had a permanent daft smile fixed on his face. He could have given Kopek a run for his money in the longest tongue contest, it was very long, and it used to flap at the side of his head as he went careening around the field. The first time we met Alfred was when he and his owner joined us on our second circuit of the field one day, asking if we minded him walking with us. Alfred's owner was limping a bit and was walking with the aid of a stick. He explained that he had recently broken his leg and was a bit worried about letting Alfred off the lead in case he didn't come back because he was in no state to run after him.

"Do you think he'll be OK off the lead with your chap?" He asked pointing at Alfred and Kopek.

"I'm sure they will be fine together," I said, "but Kopek's only a puppy, and still full of that boundless energy that puppies always seem to have," I warned.

"That's OK" He replied, "I have never seen Alfred run out of puff yet, and he's built like a train. How about recall, is he any good at that?"

I explained about Kopek's selective hearing but assured him that he had never run out of the park, so it should be safe enough. Well, he let Alfred off the lead, and he and Kopek seemed to take to each other as if they were friends of old, both of them went for a manic run around the field.

After about half an hour, we thought that we should call them back as it was time to head for home, and I had a teleconference for work. Kopek showed no sign of the minute amount of recall that we had started to train him in, and Alfred was no better I'm afraid to say. Alfred's owner was almost hoarse, by the time the pair of them decided to come back, and see what all the shouting was about. I had given up calling Kopek some time before. I had learned that when he developed selective deafness, it was pointless wasting my breath calling him back. Alfred, by this time, was totally soaked. This was due to him being rolled several times in the wet grass by Kopek, and it did not help that Kopek's mouth spent a lot of time around Alfred's neck.

The next time we met Alfred, his owner had brought a whistle. He said he had been trying to train Alfred to come back at the sound of it. He sounded quite optimistic, and he said that he'd been quite successful when he had tried it out in his back garden. As soon as Alfred was let off the lead, both he and Kopek went tearing off as usual across the field. There were about six other dogs around that day, and they all joined in, it was quite a melee. After about ten minutes, Alfred's owner started to blow his whistle to call him back, and all the dogs stopped and looked over. Alfred's owner kept blowing and blowing, his face was starting to turn a very odd shade of red. After several minutes of continuous whistles, one by one, all the dogs made their way over to Alfred's owner. All of them that is, except for Alfred and Kopek, who were far too busy, having fun on the other side of the field. As on the previous time, they both eventually came back, but that was only when they were good and ready.

One thing I have found very odd about dog owners is that they very rarely introduced themselves. Out of the dozen or so owners that Ronnie and I know from walking on the field with Kopek, I think we only know the names of about four or five of them. The rest we always refer to as Benny's mum or Bob's dad. Some of these people we have known for several years, as one of us, had spoken to them almost every day, yet we only ever refer to them through their dog's names.

Benny and Snoopy were two beagles, that while not being in the group of daily walkers, we used to meet on a regular basis. I believe they were brothers, but they were as different as chalk and cheese. Snoopy was pretty much a loner and was quite happy to run around sniffing the ground, only joining in the play occasionally. Benny, on the other hand, used to get stuck in at every opportunity, he was also somewhat enamoured of all the other dogs. At least that is the politest way I can put it. He was not what you would call discerning in his habits; he didn't seem to care about breed, shape, or size. He would simply have a bit of a sniff, and then quick as you like would start to hump. He also didn't seem to mind which end he humped, and it was a common sight to see a dog wandering around the field with Benny hanging from their head, or some other part of their anatomy.

Another one of Kopek's harem was a dog called Africa; she was a beautiful pointer that was around the same age as him. They used to bomb around the field together and seemed very well suited to each other, as far as craziness went they were as bad as each other were. Now while Kopek's recall was not the best in the world, Africa was in a league all of her own. It was a common spectacle to see her owner almost in tears, with the frustration of trying to get her to come back. I also think Africa could rival Kopek in the naughtiness stakes. There was one time that Africa's owner came on the field, half-laughing, and half-crying, saying "Naughty girl" to Africa. After asking whether she was all right, she explained that when she had let Africa out of the car by the entrance to the field, the dog had run right across the road, and straight into someone's house through the open front door. After calling her for a minute or so with no response, she had had no choice but to go in after her.

She said that the sight that greeted her was like one out of a film. She went into the house calling "Hello" every couple of steps, and when there was no response, she had ventured further in, eventually coming to the kitchen. There she saw a baby in a high chair, a mother with a spoon in her hand, and Africa vacuuming up the crumbs under the baby chair. Luckily, the mother was a dog owner and had been very understanding, so after apologising she had grabbed Africa by the scruff of her neck and dragged her out. I find it unbelievable sometimes, how some dog owners can take the most extraordinary events in their stride, and simply shrug it off saying "That's what dogs do." I believe it was just after this that Africa's owner decided to take her to dog training, classes. I was sure that Kopek would never dream of doing anything like that.

Despite my natural aversion to exercise, I was starting to enjoy walking Kopek in the morning. Ronnie and I would take it in turns, if I was working at home, or going in late I would walk him, else Ronnie would take him out. Of course, I preferred it so much more, when at the weekend, we took him somewhere where there was a pub close by to the end of the walk. I wouldn't go as far as to say I was becoming fit, but I was now walking thirty to forty miles a week. This was probably twenty-five to thirty-five more than I used to do. I thought that this achievement certainly deserved celebrating by having a pint of Guinness, or three, at the local pub. Tim, being the age he was, had required so very little exercise, that often a mile or two a day would be enough for him. At that point, he would often simply lie down, and refuse to move. One of us, normally me, would have to pick him up and carry him back to the car.

It was always interesting when a new male dog arrived on the field, especially if he was entire, (if you know what I mean). There then ensued a brief period of growling and pushing to determine who was the alpha dog. Thankfully, this never got out of control, and the worst time was a bit of 'almost fighting,' with lots of noise and gnashing of teeth, but no actual contact. As soon as another dog got a bit antsy with Kopek, he generally turned tail and ran. As he grew older, he did start to stand up for himself a bit more, but he never became aggressive. By the time, he was thirteen months old he was starting to use his 'voice' with other dogs. As he was running with them, doing his pushing thing, he would be growling away, but as his tail was permanently wagging, so he was obviously enjoying himself. The field has become very much an integral part of all our lives. It sets the mood for the whole day, if Kopek has been good, then we're a lot happier, and if he's had a good run round, then he's a lot quieter and content.

Chapter 4 - The next few months

*Kopek loves cars, but not in a nice way. Nice
cars and bad dogs just do not mix.*

I know what you are waiting for, when did Kopek get past the dog
gates? Well, he never once even tried to get over, under, or around the
gate into the lounge. But yes, he managed two out of the three with
regards to the gate at the bottom of the stairs. He never did figure a
way to get over the gates, which was surprising as they were only
three-foot-high, and he was not a small dog. I'm just over six foot, yet
he could put his paws on my chest with no effort at all, and by
stretching, he could almost reach my shoulders. He could have easily,
leapt over the gate, and into the lounge without even thinking about it.
Thankfully he never did, think about it that is.

The first thing Kopek tried to do was to dig his way under the
stair gate, but all he managed to achieve doing that was to destroy the
carpet on the bottom step. I do think that this helped to delay him
from pursuing his goal, though, as he spent the next few days keeping
himself occupied, by either digging up or eating the carpet from this
step. When digging failed to achieve his aim of getting upstairs, he
started doing some sort of gymnastics on the bottom of the gate, until
he worked the fixings loose. Two one-inch screws fixed the gate in
place at the top; these screwed into the wall on one side, and the
banister upright on the other. At the bottom, extending plastic knobs
held it in place, the ones you have to unscrew until they hold by the
opposing pressure.

I think he must have jumped against the gate, and then dug at
the bottom extender, and this combination eventually allowed him to
unscrew the bottom. This meant that he could start to explore
upstairs, by squeezing through the resulting four-inch gap. It still
amazes me to this day that for such a large dog, the size of holes that

he manages to squeeze through. I really would have loved to see this in action, but sadly, he only ever tried this when we were both out.

Apart from his gymnastics routine, there was the odd time, when one of us must have simply forgotten to close the gate properly. (Never me of course, it must have been Ronnie). During the first couple of weeks, since we had put the gates up, he managed to get up there at least four times. It was during one of these escapades, to the 'upstairs land of unlimited things to chew,' that the incident with the toilet rolls occurred. I couldn't believe how he managed to tear twenty-four rolls into such small pieces, and I thought it an amazing show of patience from a dog that had shown none up to that point. I wished he would show that same patience in other ways, but that would probably be asking too much.

You must have left the gate open

From then on, when we were out, this was something he did every time he managed to get upstairs. From what I could tell, his thought process must have gone something like the following:

1. Check no one is about
2. Create gap in gate
3. Head for the nice smelling room upstairs
4. Check no one has come home yet
5. Identify and grab the big paper roll toy
6. Run down the stairs
7. Final check for potential unwanted interference
8. Shred the paper

I have never been sure which way round he did the shredding, but the bits at the bottom of the stairs were usually wetter than the ones at the top. The end result either way would leave a layer of small paper flakes covering the floors and stairs. This behaviour resulted in us trying to remember, never to leave the toilet door open when we went out. Thankfully we were successful more often than not in this respect, and after an initial couple of weeks, this became a less common sight to come home to.

It was during another one of his forays upstairs that I think he learned that books were made of that wonderful paper stuff. Both Ronnie and I are avid book readers, and so we normally had a couple of books each, by the side of the bed. At least, I should say we used to, not after Kopek discovered they were made of paper we didn't. From then on, we kept them on top of the wardrobe, out of his way. Kopek doesn't simply eat a book, as any other self-respecting dog would do. Oh no, he only ever eats the last chapter, I don't know how he resists the rest, but he does. I have no idea why, or even how he insists on doing this, but I do wish he'd stop it. Anytime he was on his own, and he discovered a book, quick as a flash, very small, and very wet squares would be all that was left of the last dozen pages. There was one time when we were going out to see some friends, and we had decided to leave Kopek at home for an hour. Our friends liked dogs, but they had three cats, and we thought that might just be too much of a temptation for Kopek. While there was an easy truce between Kopek and Gucci, there was the odd occasion when he would decide to give her a bit of exercise by chasing her around the lounge, and we did not think our friends would appreciate their cats being exercised in this way.

We had just sat in the car when I remembered I had left the latest book I had been reading on the ledge by the front door. This ledge is where I left everything that I meant to take upstairs, and then I would then generally find that Ronnie had moved it before I got around to doing it. Her intrepid sense of tidiness meant that I couldn't leave anything out for more than a minute or so before it was 'tidied' away. "Hang on a minute," I said to Ronnie "I'd better move that book or Kopek will do his shredding routine on it." I had only been out of the house for two minutes, or at least as long as it takes to walk ten steps and get in a car. The very next page I was going to read had gone, it, along with the next twenty-seven had been shredded. He had thoughtfully left me the final thirty-nine pages, although they were a little damp. The one thing I could never figure out was how did he know where I had read up to?

I could never decide whether it was better when he did it to a book I had not yet started or one I was just about to finish. But either way, it was getting embarrassing having to go into the local bookshop to buy the same book twice in one week. I am sure they thought I was some senile old duffer, and I had forgotten that I'd already bought that book. At least if I had not yet started it, I could read something else until I could get to an out of town bookstore to replace the chewed one.

That night I simply sighed, gave him a half-hearted "Bad Kopek, bad," then turned around, shut the door and got back into the car. "At least it'll keep him occupied," I said to Ronnie, although it was more in hope than conviction.

I feel I should explain why we used to shut all the doors in the house, except for the kitchen, and our bedroom. The kitchen door we left open because that was where Kopek had his food and water bowls. We left the main bedroom door open because that was where Gucci had her bed, and she often slept in it on top of one of the wardrobes during the day. This and the lounge were her two places of sanctuary from Kopek during daylight hours. It was odd, but he almost never seemed to be interested in her during the night. Gucci had really settled during the time we had Tim, and she was often to be found simply lazing around all over the house. She went through a phase of bringing us presents, mice, birds, and on several occasions a frog or two. However, after a year she seemed to quieten down, and sleep for most of the day, only arising for meal times. She seemed to spend most of the night out of the house, doing whatever it is, that cats do during the night. Since Kopek had arrived her life had changed somewhat, he was so much more mobile than Tim was for one thing. He also had that puppy sense of inquisitiveness, and that meant he stuck his nose in lots of places that it was not really wanted. Gucci was not exempt from his nose treatment, and she was less than impressed when he would press that big wet, cold nose into places where no cat wanted a dog's nose pressed.

As I have mentioned, Kopek and Gucci have an odd rapport, one of those that could truly be described as a love-hate relationship. There are days when I see them both curled up together, Gucci content, tucked inside Kopek's legs. But then there are other days when he just keeps chasing her around the house. Alternatively, he will persistently shove his nose into her while she was lying on the sofa. If he ever does the latter when she is asleep, the response is quite dramatic. Gucci will come awake in an instant, with a shocked look on her face (wouldn't you with a cold, wet nose shoved up your backside), and all four legs will shoot out. She will then try to fix as many claws as she can into Kopek's face. I'm sure that most other dogs would head for the hills at this point, but not Kopek. He will simply back up a step or two, shake his head, and then shove his nose back in again for seconds. I have seen Kopek standing with Gucci hanging freely from his head, it must have hurt him, but he didn't seem to be bothered. It was a case of 'Where's there's no sense...' I suppose.

One day I had to go into work for a couple of hours, and I was a little apprehensive, as two hours was a lot of time for Kopek to do his search and destroy routine with our possessions. I dismissed my feelings of unease, even if he did manage to make it upstairs, I had checked that all the doors were closed, except for the ones to our bedroom, and how much damage could he do in there? Kopek chose this day, for his 'piece de resistance' in the destruction stakes so far. When I opened the front door, there he was, with his happy smiling face, tongue lolling, tail wagging, and no sign of destruction. That was apart from the local free paper, but as that was now a once weekly occurrence, we had become used to this. We called it his 'Paper Mangling Tuesday' (PMT). He just loves that paper, and he had done his usual trick of reducing it into a fair imitation of snow. "Oh well," I thought "Not too bad." I didn't even bother to admonish him, as it was a pointless gesture. He knew it, and I knew it. There was no way he was ever going to allow a newspaper to lay on the floor, and not shred it. He gave me a look as if to say, "Oh come on, you knew it was Tuesday, and you went out and left me alone. What did you honestly expect me to do?"

So feeling quite happy and relieved, I gave him ten minutes of play, while I put the kettle on for a mug of coffee. It was about fifteen minutes later when I had cause to go upstairs, that I had that really unpleasant sinking feeling in my stomach. The bedroom door was slightly ajar, which was normal, but I could see a few feathers on the bedroom floor, and that was most definitely not normal. "What's that?" I asked myself aloud. At the sound of my raised voice, Kopek slunk down the stairs in stealth mode. I stuck my head round the door, with an impending sense of doom. I had never seen a sight of so much destruction in my life. There, in what was normally a very tidy bedroom, was a scene of total Armageddon. It looked like he had jumped on the bed and decided to see if he could dig his way through, maybe he thought there was some big monster he needed to destroy. Two feather pillows, the duvet, and oh yes, the mattress, along with the bottom bed sheet were completely shredded. All I can say, it's a good job George W Bush had never heard of Kopek, or else we would have had the US Marines knocking on the door before you could say 'Weapons of Mass Destruction.'

To say I was annoyed would have been a tad of an understatement. I shot out of the bedroom and down the stairs to get him, and there ensued a game of 'Catch the Hound.' I had gained a lot of experience in this game since getting Kopek, but he still had the edge over me. After ten minutes of chasing him around the hall and kitchen, he spotted a space and darted through my legs. He then shot up the stairs, with me in hot pursuit. He dived straight for the bedroom, and I followed him through, shutting the door triumphantly behind me. I managed to corner him at one end of the bedroom then dived, catching him in a rugby tackle. "Gotcha, you little bugger." Only to find, that all I ended up with was an armful of his fur. I learned just how amazingly wriggly a dog could be. He managed to squirm out of my arms and squeezed under the bed.

Kopek had grown to a fair size at this point, so he could only fit under the bed by lying on his stomach, with his back legs sprawled out behind him, and his front ones drawn up under his chest. I got the feeling that he was really starting to enjoy himself at this point, and that the fun had overtaken the fear. As I would try and reach him on one side, he would sort of shuffle along on his stomach, over to the other side. It was pointless grabbing hold of one part of him, as I knew all I would end up with, was a face full of dog foot. I needed to try to corner him somehow, so all I could do at that juncture was to attempt to herd him out from under the bed. At one point, while I was having a brief rest, panting half under the bed, I saw him take a stray piece of the bed sheet in his mouth and start toying with it.

"That's it" I shouted, my blood pressure was rising to a probable dangerous level. I then spent the next fifteen minutes herding, diving, and grabbing until I finally had him by the scruff of his neck. I dragged him over to a large pile of feathers and pushed his nose into what remained of one of the pillows. "What's this?" I shouted at him. "What have you done?" Why, when talking to animals, do we state the obvious? I already knew the answers to these questions, but somehow shouting them at Kopek, made me feel better. He looked at me as if to say, "Not me Guv, it must've been some other dog. I wasn't even here." This with feathers stuck all over his face. I relented. I must admit despite my being so annoyed, I couldn't stay mad at him for very long, he only had to give me those soulful eyes, along with that daft lolling tongue, and my annoyance somehow drifted away.

After that began the long task of cleaning up, filling a black bin bag with the remnants of the pillows and bed sheet, and another with the remains of the duvet. I must have filled two vacuum bags trying to clear up all the feathers, and even so, we were still finding stray feathers for months after. Wistfully I thought back to the salesman in the bed shop proudly telling us that 'this mattress will give you years of service and comfort.' "Not when you own a dog it won't," I thought to myself ruefully. Thankfully it was an expensive mattress, I say that not to be perverse, but it did mean that I was able to turn it over, and it still remained solid enough to continue giving us a comfortable night's sleep. I looked at Kopek and gave him one last admonishment. He looked at me turning his head on one side then the other and then seemed to try another tack with "I'm sure I could smell a bone in there somewhere. Is it time for a walk yet?"

The infamous Tongue

Well, we had had an interesting few months, and we had learned quite a few things about Kopek. He was no longer quite so manic on opening the front door, and in recent weeks, he had lulled us into a false sense of security, in that two out of every three times he was left, he was the perfect picture of a well-behaved dog. It was now more common to come home to find him simply curled up asleep than to find what resembled the aftermath of an episode of Tom and Jerry. However, on that one in three occasions, he went to town. His latest achievement was my car.

I used to buy a car for about a thousand pounds, or less if I could find a real bargain. I would then run it into the ground over a period of two years, give or take six months. I always tried to buy the best car I could find and using this method, I have owned quite a few beautiful cars, Lancia, Jaguar, and Daimler, to name a few. I once managed to buy a Lancia Beta for two hundred and fifty pounds; it was quite a rust bucket, but it lasted me for over six months and was such a fun car to drive.

The best car I had bought so far, using this method, was a 1988 Jaguar XJ12, the one with the five point three engine and twelve cylinders. I paid a little more than normal for this, as it was in such great condition, but even so, I managed to pick it up for twelve hundred pounds. Apart from the usual small amount of rust around the windscreen, the bodywork was in pretty good condition, and it was a beautiful British Racing Green. Just listening to that twelve-cylinder engine made me go all Jeremy Clarkson, and driving it just put a great big smile on my face. This had been my pride and joy and was such a comfortable car that we drove to Turkey and back in it over a three-week period. Unfortunately, it started to develop electrical problems, and that was the time to get rid of it, but it had lasted me nearly two years and gave me miles of fun. However, my latest fun car at that time was a 1992 Range Rover, with all the trimmings, that I had picked up for a princely sum of seven hundred and fifty pounds. I wouldn't want to give the impression that I had 'Loadsa Money,' but, as I tended not to drive too many miles, I could, as a rule, trade the high fuel consumption against the other low running costs.

The first couple of times we left Kopek in the car while we went shopping, he was fine. We would arrive back at the car to find him sitting in the driver's seat, peacefully watching the world go by. He had his bowl of water, a toy, and/or bone to keep him occupied, and this seemed to keep him happy and relaxed. He had a definite preference to being left in the car, rather than being on his own at home. I think it was the third time that he had been left for about thirty minutes, that we came back to the car to find he had helped himself to frissons of plastic, such as the indicator stalks, along with the light switches on the dashboard. The next occasion something like this happened, he had helped himself to the steering wheel. I can tell you it was rather uncomfortable, trying to steer the car with a steering wheel that is missing chunks of all but a band of steel.

I had had enough, and I was considering getting a dog guard at this point. I didn't want to pay for a proper Range Rover one, as that would probably have cost more than the car was worth. So I decided that I would go to Halfords, and get a cheap multi-car one. But first I had to go into town and buy a book, this was to replace the one Kopek had eaten earlier in the week. I didn't want to leave Kopek in the house alone, as the whole trip would take me over an hour, so I decided to take him with me. The bookshop was not far from the car park, and I had only been gone for half an hour at the most, as I knew exactly what book I was buying. I was walking back to the car thinking "off to Halfords, and then perhaps there's time for a quick pint in the local." I must confess, I was feeling quite smug at the thought of finally getting one over on Kopek, and stopping him from eating any more of my car. When I got back to the car, he had eaten the front seat. I'm not talking about a little chew of the fabric you understand, but big chunks of the foam as well. There he was sitting quite happily on the passenger seat. When I unlocked the car, he looked at me as if to say, "You're going to have to do something about that seat. It's just not comfortable to sit on anymore." Needless to say, I didn't bother going to Halfords, but instead went straight to the pub and had several pints of Guinness.

The Remains

Chapter 7 - Out and about

Enough was enough, and that was the final straw, the car, by this time, was looking tired in the extreme, especially as in the last two weeks, the sunroof had sprung a leak. We decided it was time to ditch the Range Rover, and buy something that had more of a prison cell in the back, one that could house a category 'A' prisoner. So Ronnie and I had a long chinwag and decided to go for something solid, safe, and supposedly indestructible. That's right, a Volvo. Admittedly, not as nice a car as I was used to, but it was certainly economical and roomy. But to be honest, the real reason I didn't mind giving up on a fun car, was that I just could not bear the thought of buying a really nice one and knowing it was only going to be a matter of time before Kopek would eat his way through it. After a couple of weeks of researching Volvos, I found a nice cheap V40 going for auction on eBay. I had always found that you could get some good bargains on eBay if you knew exactly what you were looking for, and I had done my homework. I managed to win the auction with a bid of twelve hundred and twelve pounds, for a two thousand X-reg model. As it only had eighty-six thousand miles on the clock and had most of its service history, I thought it was a very good price. The car was in Portsmouth, so after contacting the seller and arranging when would be convenient, I decided to let the train take the strain and go down the next day.

Kopek had never been on a train before, so I thought it might be fun to take him with me. Also, Ronnie was going to be out at work all day, so there was never any question of leaving him on his own in the house for that length of time. God knows what he would have got up to in order keep himself entertained for a whole day; it just did not bear thinking about. The plan was to take the train from Suffolk to London, then go on the underground, and finally on to Portsmouth on a straight through the train. The seller of the car had kindly offered to pick us both up at Portsmouth station, so there were no worries about finding his house at the other end.

The next morning I turned up bright and early at the train station. I wasn't sure whether I'd have to pay for Kopek or not, so rather than buying a ticket on-line, I queued up at the ticket office. For some reason, there was a quite a queue, and Kopek was showing just how bad a dog he could be. Twice I had to give him a sharp jerk on his lead; he had that look about him, the one he gets just before he has a pee. He would then look at me as though to say "Ah c'mon dad, I really need to mark my turf you know." I was praying that the chaps in their business suits didn't notice the huge amount of hair that Kopek was leaving on their trouser legs.

"I need to get to Portsmouth," I told the teller when my turn at the desk finally arrived. "Do I need to pay for him?"

"No, he's free, but for you, the price is a mere fifty-six pounds."

Great, a comedian, just what I needed in my mood. "Bloody hell, that's a bit steep isn't it?"

"Yes, sorry. If you'd booked in advance it would only have been thirty-five pounds, you could have even gone first class for forty-three pounds."

Don't you just hate that, when people tell you what you could have had. It's like that TV programme Bullseye. Jim Bowen would say to the poor loser "Here's what you could have won." Showing them a boat or a car, before presenting them with a pen or some such trinket.

"OK, I'll take it," I said, "Is that the two stopper?"

"Yes, you change at Liverpool Street for the Underground to Waterloo, then on a straight through train to Portsmouth and Southsea. Do you want a timetable?"

"I suppose I'd better," I said, "I might get held up in London with this fella."

"Here you go. You've probably read this one, but there's a new one out next week. It's sure to hit the best sellers list." He passed over the latest edition of the timetable. Despite my mood, this made me smile; the old ones are the best.

The journey to London Liverpool St. gave me great comfort in that it was uneventful, and this was despite Kopek insisting on sitting on his own seat and staring out the window. I did try to keep him on the floor, but he wasn't having any of it, and I soon gave up wrestling with him. I think he just couldn't bear not being able to look out of the window and watch the world pass by. I was a little surprised, but the ticket inspector didn't seem to mind him sitting on the seats, so I gave up, and let him win that one. I was beginning to understand, that the trick with Kopek was to forget about some of the battles but concentrate on trying to win the war. On arriving in London, I thought better of trying to take Kopek on the Underground, it was getting close to Christmas, and there were large crowds everywhere. While the train down had been relatively quiet, this would be a completely different ball game, and I didn't fancy carrying him up and down the escalators, to be honest.

I decided to take a taxi across town to Waterloo station, where I was to catch the next train onto Portsmouth. The taxi driver loved Kopek; he had never seen a British-Inuit before, and so there were many questions about his breed and his characteristics. The driver had two dogs of his own, both of which were boxers, and I'm sure you know what it is like when two dog lovers start talking about dogs. The journey across town was filled with lots of dog topic conversation, each of us comparing stories about what our dogs got up to. We arrived at

Waterloo in what seemed like minutes, and I was relieved that Kopek had refrained from seeing what a London taxi tasted like.

The train journey to Portsmouth was a lot more interesting, to say the least. There were a few more people on the train than had been on the one down to London, but it was by no means crowded. There was an elderly gentleman sitting on the seat that backed onto the one where Kopek had staked his claim. He was a particularly well-dressed man, with a dapper suit, and an air of the military about him. All of a sudden, Kopek stopped looking outside and started to take an extraordinary interest in the gentleman's hat. It was one of those Trilby type ones. Thank goodness, the man seemed to like Kopek, he had half turned round and was talking to him in that way that people talk to dogs. "Oh, you're a nice looking fellow aren't you?" And "What a handsome chap you are." He was giving Kopek's head and ears a rub, while at the same time, trying to keep his head away from Kopek's mouth. Quick as a flash, Kopek snatched the gentleman's hat off his head and jumped onto the floor. I'm sure that wouldn't have been so bad, except that Kopek had also taken the man's wig with it. Apologising will only let you get away with so much, and as usual with Kopek, this was way beyond so much. I'm afraid I played the chicken and pretended to get off at the next stop, which the train was luckily fast approaching. I snuck back on the next but one carriage further down the train, desperately hoping that the gentleman had not noticed us.

If there is one thing that dogs can excel at that, it's their innate ability to take you to the absolute extremes of embarrassment. After a big admonishment, and keeping him on a very short lead on the floor as punishment, Kopek settled down somewhat. I have quite long legs, so I generally stretch them out in the aisle if I can when I'm travelling on the train. Why is it that as soon as you get in a comfortable position, the food trolley comes down the aisle? It's the same on aeroplanes, you just about manage to get to sleep, because you have spent the last fifteen hours in the airport due to delays, and you get: "Excuse me, sir, would you care for any duty-free?" I'm sure they do it on purpose. Anyway, after drawing my legs back in and dragging Kopek back into the space between the seats, I politely declined any of the delightful offerings of the trolley, and it rolled on past. It was a minute or so later, on hearing some rustling, I looked down and noticed Kopek munching his way through a packet of crisps. He must have snatched them off the bottom of the trolley as it passed. I gave him the look, the one that says, "What am I going to do with you?" He gave me the look back that said "What? Did you want a crisp?"

I gave thanks that the remaining journey was without incident, and we duly arrived at Portsmouth station. We then alighted from the train and walked down the platform, heading for the car park where the seller of the Volvo had arranged to meet us. It was as I was waiting for Kopek to finish his lengthy pee against a bin that I looked to my right at the train as it was pulling out, there I saw the elderly gentleman staring out of his window shaking his fist. "Oh well, so much for the train taking the strain," I thought to myself. We met up with the seller, whose name was Jim, in the car park as arranged, and headed off to his house to see the car. Jim's wife kindly offered to look after Kopek, while I took the car for a test drive with Jim. I was a little nervous about leaving him, not because I didn't trust Jim's wife, but at the thought of what havoc Kopek might cause while I was away. Nevertheless, Jim's wife assured me that she would be fine. After some last-minute warnings about not letting him near anything made of paper, I jumped in the car, and we set off.

I was very happy with the car; it handled really well and was extremely comfortable. So when we arrived back at Jim's house, I handed the cash over and collected Kopek. Amazingly, he had been on his best behaviour, either that or Jim's wife was extremely polite and didn't want to tell me what he'd been up to. I put Kopek in the boot; it was an estate after all, although after his recent behaviour I might have been tempted even if it wasn't. I then set off for the drive back home to Suffolk, and fortunately, the journey was a lot quicker by car than by train. I was happy the drive home was quiet because I didn't think I could take much more excitement that day. There was only one point of note, and that was when I stopped the car to let Kopek out for a pee break at a motorway service station. As it was quiet, I had let him off the lead in a grassed area, and close by were some schoolchildren sat on wooden benches. I was fully occupied keeping a watch out for any other dogs that might make an appearance; I didn't want Kopek going off to play, as I wouldn't have got him to come back for at least half an hour if that happened. I heard a big "Ah, Look at him. Isn't he cute," from behind me, the kids had noticed Kopek and were admiring him. Then I heard "Eeew. That's disgusting."

I knew exactly what had happened; Kopek had decided that he needed more than a pee and had proudly created some sort of sculpture. I thought it was quite amusing personally, but then I do have a bit of a warped sense of humour. Bagging it up, I thought how lucky I had been that he had managed not to do this on the train. Once home, I showed the new car off to Ronnie. "Look at how well it's been kept," I said. Ronnie was having a good look in the back of the car, checking the legroom, and rear seats. She suddenly stuck her head up and asked, "What's that? What's wrong with the rear seat belt holder?" Yes, Kopek had obviously become bored on the return journey and had a little nibble to while away the hours.

The morning after buying the Volvo, Ronnie and I went off to Halfords. I wonder if the town planners had intended it, but Halfords is just across the road from Pets at Home. Perhaps the planners were dog owners and knew just how useful it would be to have these two stores in close proximity to each other. Toys to keep your dog from chewing your car, but just in case that doesn't work, just over the road, you can purchase the replacement car parts that your dog used as a toy. I was determined not to give Kopek any chance of repeating his Range Rover feats. We had gone there to purchase one of those "one size fits all" dog guards. Let me tell you right now, they don't. Not even if you follow all the instructions to the letter. You know the ones, I'm sure a bunch of schoolchildren first translates them from Korean, and then someone adds random words and then takes out all the punctuation marks. 'Twisting and pull/push both sections of C whistle inserting it into section A, make sure keep you holding of section E that fit then you to section A.' The fact was, there was no section C, and even if there was, there was nowhere in section A to insert it into. Despite this, and the fact I don't have the three hands that seemed to be required, I did manage to assemble it. I was quite proud of myself. I had lost a stone in weight and had fingers that looked as though they had been rubbed vigorously against a cheese grater, but I had beaten it. I did a little dance of celebration around the car, punching the air with both bloody hands, much to Ronnie's embarrassment. However, I didn't care, I had won, and there it was fitted into the back of the Volvo.

I do believe I heard a smattering of applause, from the crowd that had gathered in Halford's car park, to watch the crazy, swearing man, assemble his new dog guard. It was maybe not quite straight, and there were a few unexpected gaps around the edges. Nevertheless, nothing larger than a couple of inches, and surely nothing big enough that Kopek could possibly squeeze through. "Solid as a rock, no way he's going to get through that," I claimed to Ronnie, my voice filled with pride. So we put Kopek back in the boot, he was most intrigued by the new dog guard and was sniffing it all over, we got in the front, and we set off homeward. On the way home, I checked my rearview mirror to find it full of a tongue lolling out of a very happy furry face, as Kopek sat on the back seat. He must have been in stealth mode because neither of us had heard a thing.

When we arrived home, I inspected the dog guard a little more closely. He must have gotten a bit peckish because he had eaten the plastic bits that hold the mesh to the poles if you follow my drift. This, along with the looseness of one side, had allowed him to slide between the side rear window and the dislodged meshing. "It's OK, they're only there for support," I said to Ronnie while repositioning the guard more firmly against the back headrests, and giving the screws one extra twist. Actually, they are not. If you don't have them, a medium sized Houdini inclined dog can squeeze through the four-inch gap they allow between the mesh and the bars. This is what happened when we left him the next day. Thankfully he must have been full (probably from eating the latest book I'd been reading), because he was quite happily sitting in the driver's seat, watching the world go by, as we arrived back at the car.

Lots of wire ties and persistence later, and the dog guard was finally secured properly. Moreover, it actually did the job. He did manage to eat both legs off it, you know the ones you "simply twist and push/pull to make it fit comfortably to the floor of the car." He also managed to chew the back off the middle rear headrest, but on the whole, it performed the job of keeping him in the boot. God help us if we ever had to remove it, though, because it is somehow jammed between the headrests, the actual seats, and the back windows, and it is never, ever, going to come out again. I had noticed an odd thing about Kopek if we put something in place to try to secure him; he seemed to take this as some sort of challenge. If he successfully managed to negotiate the dog guard or gate, he would often just be sitting quietly waiting for us to get back.

The Infamous Dog Guard

Chapter 5 - The escapologist

With his daring feats of escapes, Harry Houdini was widely regarded as one of the greatest escapologists in history. I think Kopek may just have exceeded him.

Over the next few months, things settled into a predictable routine, and although the occasions Kopek went on the rampage were getting less often, we still never lost that feeling of trepidation when we left him. When we had to leave Kopek on his own in the house, we would play the game of "guess the object." This is a simple game. Ronnie and I would try to guess, what treasured object he would have eaten while we were out. One thing neither of us guessed was the Universe.

I think I will have to explain. You know those adverts on the TV for magazines, with collect all these parts, and you can build your own Formula 1 replica car (note: scaled model only), part one only 99p (normal price £550 a month for the rest of your life). Well, as you may have guessed by now, I am just a little impulsive, and I had seen one of these advertisements for "Build your own Universe." It looked quite cool, with brass parts, and many fiddly cogs, so I sent off for it and signed up for the series. I eagerly awaited the first delivery, and two weeks later it arrived, three issues all at the same time. It was unfortunate, but Kopek arrived a little earlier than I did that day, and when I arrived back home, he had gone to work on it. I swear I'm not making this up. He managed to open the package and take great care to eat three pages out of one of the magazines, and those were the exact three pages, on which the instructions on how to put part one of my Universe together were on. There he was, sitting 'Happy as Larry', looking exceptionally pleased with what he had done. "Look, dad, I unpacked it for you."

If anyone has the same affliction as me and bought this series, could you please send me a copy of those instructions. It would be interesting to know whether I got it right. I do sometimes wonder how much of the Universe I'm going to have to build before they stop sending, and charging, me for the magazines. I'm up to issue forty-six so far. I do hope that it will end soon, and it will not be one of those Universes that simply go on forever, as I don't want to have to try to cancel the subscription.

When I was younger, I subscribed to Readers Digest, a magazine that had enticed me with promises of articles filled with so much information that I couldn't possibly go through life without. For the first five or six months, all was well, and I have to admit to enjoying the magazines, but then other stuff started arriving through my letter box. You Have Won One Million Pounds, or really the chance to enter our competition to win one million pounds. Others were offers of either more magazines or books with exciting titles, such as The Readers Digest Guide to First Aid. It had started to get to the point when every time the post arrived; there was a deluge of absolutely useless mail, which far outweighed any post that was of interest. So I decided to cancel my subscription and make sure that I got my name off their database. I wonder if anyone has ever been successful in cancelling a Readers Digest subscription.

It's not just them; I think most subscriptions are the same; they just refuse to let you go. I rang them up, and then I sent them letters, but they kept on sending me not just the magazine, but all the other paraphernalia as well. I begged and pleaded with them, and they would be very polite and say, "Of course Mr. Owens, we'll cancel that right away for you." The next month, I heard the dreaded thump on the doormat of the magazine arriving. In the end, I found the only way to really stop these people, was to move house. It may not have stopped them delivering it, but at least I could rest assured in the knowledge that they no longer had my address. I have sometimes felt a twinge of remorse for the person who bought my old house. But then I think back to the near heart attack I had with the frustration and think, "What the hell."

By the time that Kopek had reached his tenth month on this Earth, he was developing into the Houdini of the canine world. It was around this time that Kopek learned the wonderful trick of opening the front door. We have one of those double-glazed doors, which have a simple lever on the inside, so all it needs is some downward pressure, and the door will open. I came home from work one afternoon to find no dog, and a note pushed through the letterbox. The fact that the note was still there, and not shredded into small pieces, testified to the fact that Kopek was probably not home. I unfolded the note and started to read:

Dear Phil,

My name is Sal, and I live three doors down from you. Today I saw Kopek running past the house, on his way to the park. I managed to catch him and put him back in the house, he really does like the park doesn't he. Unfortunately, 10 minutes later I saw him again, on his was back to the park. Thinking I hadn't closed the door properly, I brought him back and made sure I had firmly closed the door. After the third time, I thought it best if I kept hold of him for you, until you got back from work.

Cheers
Sal

Sal was the daughter of my neighbour, Sam, and of Elle and Miya's family, and I was thankful that she was so understanding. And so after lots of embarrassing "sorry's,'" and "Thank you's," I manhandled Kopek back to the house, with a few well-worn phrases,

"Bad Boy," and "Naughty." He just kept looking at me, with that daft tongue hanging almost to the floor. Ignorant of the amount of trouble he had caused, he was blissfully happy having spent the afternoon playing with Miya. Since then, if we ever left the front door unlocked when we left the house, we would often find ourselves shadowed by him within about five seconds. Sometimes he waited a while, other times he followed us straight out. Needless to say, there is now a big reminder by our front door; DON'T FORGET TO LOCK IT. Several further occasions someone forgot to lock the door on the way out of the house (I would like to say that it was never me, but unfortunately, I can't). One day I left the house just to go to the shops, I opened the car door, only to have Kopek jump in before me. He sat on the front seat and looked at me as if to say, "That was lucky, you nearly forgot me. Where are we going? Is it the park?"

It had now become a not uncommon occurrence, for me to get a phone call at work from one of the neighbours, just to let me know that Kopek had escaped, again. The result of this was that Kopek was becoming a hot topic of conversation among my work colleagues. So much so, that often the first thing they would eagerly ask me in the morning was, "What's the hound been up to today then?" There was an extreme disappointment if there was no tale to tell, but then that didn't happen very often. On receiving one of these phone calls, I would have to rush home, and head straight over to the park (where else?), where I would then play the game of 'Catch the Hound.' Obviously, this was a much harder game in the field than the house, due to the amount of space Kopek had to manoeuvre in.

As I walked towards him, shouting "stay," and "wait." He would sit down and wait; the perfect picture of an obedient dog. That was until I was within about ten feet of him, and then he would lope off a further twenty or thirty feet away. He would also use the trees to great effect, putting them between him and me, sniffing around just waiting for me to get near him again. It would generally take me at least half an hour to catch him, and that was only successful because he had grown tired of the game, and wanted taking home so he could have a drink and a rest. It took quite a while for us to get into the habit of locking the doors behind us, but in time, it was only on the odd occasion when one of us would forget.

There was one occasion when Kopek had escaped to the field when he came across a cat, which was sitting bold as brass on the grass giving herself a wash. Despite the fact that Kopek lives with Gucci, he is fascinated by other cats and always insists on going on in for a sniff. Well this cat was having none of it, and every time Kopek came too near, she would hiss and spit at him. He would then run away a few feet, before going back in for another attempt. This cat was well known to most of the regular dog walkers on the field; it lived in a house by one of the entrances. It was a regular sight to see her walking along, without a care in the world, all the way across the field to one her favourite sleeping spots. This was a bench within the kiddie's play area, where she would stretch out in the sun.

Kopek Playing hide and seek in the Trees

This was not turning out to be a good day, as I now knew I now had no chance of catching Kopek, not while the cat remained on the field, taunting him. I had to admit, he certainly showed persistence and a lot of courage, either that or it was simply his inane stupidity that kept him at it for twenty-five minutes. It went on and on, with the same thing happening repeatedly, it was like watching a short film on a loop. He would run around the cat in circles, getting ever closer and closer, then the cat would make a lunge at him, and he would run away a few feet, with his tail between his legs. Then he would start all over again. Finally, the cat had had enough, and quickly but regally, trotted off to her bench within the fenced area, where she promptly curled up and went to sleep.

Kopek was so tired out after all this cavorting about that he meekly let me put the lead on him and take him straight home. Once there, he drank about a gallon of water and promptly went to sleep for the rest of the afternoon. Kopek was to meet this cat again several months later, this time it was slightly different, in that he was a bit older and a bit more confident. He had won a few battles with Gucci by then. This time, despite the hissing and lunging, Kopek carried straight on barrelling towards the cat. Realising that Kopek was not going to stop, the cat made a dash for it. It was a close thing, but she managed to just beat him to the kiddies' area by about two feet. Unfortunately, he had built up so much momentum, which he simply crashed into the railings unable to stop in time. I had only just arrived on the field, dashing straight from work, so he was still fresh and full of energy. This meant we spent another twenty minutes or so, playing ring around the play area, with Kopek barking at the cat every time he passed the bench. This time I was rescued by another dog walker, I don't think it had entered Kopek's head, that someone else might actually grab hold of him, as he was so busy trying to avoid me.

As the back door opened in a similar way to the front one, it was not long before Kopek learned how to open that one as well. This door was slightly trickier, in that it didn't swing open when he jumped on the handle, so he then had to wrap his claws around the edge to open it. However, this soon became child's play for him, and he would often let himself in and out when he fancied a bit of variety. I wonder if it's that canine Alzheimer's thing that means dogs never seem to learn how to shut doors. Do they forget that it was them that had opened them in the first place? More likely, it is just that they don't care.

Kopek has a thing for grass, and he just loves to lie on it, even when it was quite cold outside. I think it must be a thing with Northern type dogs, as I have heard from a few other owners that their dogs do the same, it's probably due to their thick double coats. When we gave Kopek a bone, the first thing he would do was to open the back door and take it out on the lawn. He would then spend half an hour chewing it and trying to get the marrow out. It was a very rare occasion when he brought the bone inside. This was one of his good traits as far as Ronnie was concerned, as she was not overly fond of having big old smelly bones in the house.

One of the funniest sights I have seen, concerning Kopek's behaviour, was when he encountered snow for the first time. We had had a heavy snowfall overnight, and the back garden was covered to a depth of about two inches. I let Kopek out so he could do his morning business, and as usual, he shot out the back door as if fired from a gun. It quickly dawned on him that something was amiss, especially on doing one of his handbrake turns he ended up flat on his face. Once he had got back up and shaken the snow off, he remembered he had a bone out there somewhere. He started trotting round the garden looking for it, but obviously, it was well and truly buried under the snow so that he couldn't locate it. What he did next, was to shove his nose into the snow, and start to plough along the ground. Every now and then, he would lift his head up and give an almighty sneeze, making the snow blow up in a cloud around him. Then his nose would go back down, and he would till another meandering furrow. He was one happy dog when he finally discovered the missing bone; around him was a wonderfully crafted maze of trails in the snow. He then destroyed these by doing a crazy run around in celebration. When we took him over to the field that morning it was a sight to behold, there must have been three or four dogs of about the same age as Kopek, that had never seen snow before, and their crazy antics went up another level altogether. There were times when it was like watching small tornadoes tearing around the field. Because they were running so fast, and furiously, you could hardly see the dogs through the blizzards they were stirring up around them.

The first Snow

Kopek also learned how to open the internal kitchen door, and that I can tell you, was no mean feat. Unless it was slammed, the door doesn't quite shut properly. It did half shut, jamming solidly enough in the frame to keep Kopek in; that was until this juncture. Somehow, by a combination of bouncing against the bottom of the door, and digging between the door and the frame he would manage to open it. Wherever we went around the house, Kopek would follow us, stuck to our legs like a piece of Velcro. Having a dog follow you everywhere, can be a little annoying, especially when you try to go to the loo or have a bath. Up to that point, we could shut him in the kitchen, secure in the knowledge that this would hold him until we had finished vacuuming or whatever. Sadly, this was no longer the case. Once he had learned that the door would open if he were persistent enough, it became our equivalent of a fire door. What I mean by this, is that it generally kept him occupied for about ten minutes before he managed to break through. It became a common sight for one of us to shut Kopek in the kitchen, and then run for the loo before the ten minutes were up. So, as well as 'catch the hound,' we now had numerous other games that we 'played' with Kopek. One I am sure many dog owners are familiar with is 'fun time with the vacuum cleaner.'

What is it about vacuum cleaners and dogs? Why do they make them go into a manic frenzy the minute they catch sight of one? Using the vacuum with Kopek around seemed to be a pointless task. For every hair that we managed to pick up, he shed at least two more, with his racing up and down. As the vacuum caused a lot of this racing, I often thought that this was simply some form of job creation. I would have given up vacuuming years ago, but Ronnie would have none of it. Kopek's breed is only supposed to moult twice a year. I think what this really means, is that twice a year he sheds two ton of hair, rather than the normal one. It's a common sight to see hairballs rolling across the wooden floors, reminiscent of a Western town and its brush balls rolling through the deserted streets.

We had a pull along cleaner, one of those that comes with hundreds of attachments that you think would be so useful when you bought it, but have never got around to using, and probably never will. I'm not sure which Kopek seemed to enjoy more, attacking it by chewing the wheels, biting the tube, or mangling the head. Alternatively, it could have been when he tried to make puppies with it. He only tried the making puppies' thing once while it was on. He gave a small yelp and shot off into the lounge. It had been on for about half an hour, and I think it may have been a little too warm for some of his more delicate parts. After that, he only tried to give it a good seeing to it if it has been left out for a while and had cooled down. As the vacuum was being wheeled around, he would pounce and grip onto one of the wheels with his teeth, other times he would attack the suction end. Apart from the shedding of hair, it really was quite difficult to vacuum with a dog attached to some part of the cleaner.

We went through three vacuum cleaners due to Kopeks ministrations. The first one simply died because it just couldn't handle the massive quantities of hair. It finally overheated and started emitting large quantities of smoke, and after that, it wouldn't even switch on. The second cleaner we bought was a bit more substantial. If it was going to have to cope with the amount of hair that one would normally only expect from a medium sized Yak, then it was going to have to be the Tonka of vacuum cleaners. Unfortunately, because it was bigger, this meant there was more of it for Kopek to chew. We got rid of that one when the wheels wouldn't go round anymore. This was because he had pretty much chewed them off, and it is really quite difficult dragging a wheeless vacuum cleaner around the house. The last one was the Hummer of the vacuum cleaning world, and it lasted almost three months. We were starting to think that we had finally beaten him, and found something that was tougher than he was. However, that was until on one of his escapades upstairs, he came face to face with it, just him and it. With no human around for protection, it didn't stand a chance. One of us had forgotten to put it away in the cupboard (probably Ronnie), and I'm pretty sure he had his evil way with it because it was covered in dog lick. At least I hoped it was dog lick. That was not the real problem, though, as you can always clean that stuff off. The issue was that Kopek had taken offence with the long flexi-tubing, and this had numerous puncture marks where he'd been arguing with it, and he had bitten right through. I was determined that the dog would not beat me again, so I used Gaffer tape to repair as many of the holes as I could. It did last a further month before we were finally forced to get another one, but that was only due to him succeeding in chewing the wheels off. We are now resigned to the fact, that any vacuum cleaner will only last an average of three months before we need to replace it.

I wouldn't want to give the impression that Kopek went on a rampage of destruction every time he was on his own. He was slowly growing up and becoming a bit more responsible as he grew older. We could now leave him on his own for an hour or two, quite often with no problems at all. But every now and then, he decided he was bored and felt the need to entertain himself. Although the frequency grew less, the resulting damage was greater. I think because it was now becoming infrequent, when it did happen, the experience was all the more shocking. During the occasions he was not pretending to be a good dog, he was either escaping through the front door, or he was entertaining himself elsewhere in the house. I was not sure which one of these things I liked the least. When he escaped out the house, I had to drop everything at work and rush home straight away. However, when he managed to get upstairs it tended to cost us money, and it generally took a lot of effort to clean up. It had reached the point where I had had to screw the dog gate, at the bottom of the stairs, in with six-inch screws, as he could work the smaller screws loose with his dog gymnastics. Despite this, if I didn't check the screws every few days, he was still able to work them loose enough that he could squeeze through the space between the bottom step, and the bottom of the gate.

A lot of the time when he did manage to get upstairs he simply went to sleep in the bedroom until one of us came home. However, when he did go on one of his destruction derbies, the results were pretty spectacular. During the following months, he had three further attempts to destroy the bed, and each time the very least he did was to shred the duvet cover and the bottom bed sheet. On two of the occasions, we were fortunate in so far as he didn't have a go at the pillows. Apart from the cost, the pillows were an absolute nightmare to clean up; we were still finding feathers from the first episode. He still hadn't managed to destroy the mattress enough that we needed a new one yet, so in some ways that salesman was right. It was still giving us plenty of support during the night, although now it did have a slight dip in the middle. One thing he did manage to do was shred the duvets every time he attacked the bed, and it was becoming a real pain. As I have never had very good taste in bed coverings, according to Ronnie that is, it was up to her to go and buy the replacement duvet.

To replace the duvet, Ronnie went to a shop called Denhelm, a general household shop, which curiously enough is near to Halfords and Pets at Home. On her last visit, the sales assistant was giving her a peculiar look. "Look, I know this is the third time I've been in here in six weeks. And I know this is the third set of bed clothes I've bought" Ronnie explained to the assistant "But honestly, I don't run a brothel, it's just that my dog has developed a taste in duvet sets." I'm not sure whether the sales assistant believed her, but she gave Ronnie a smile and helpfully pointed her in the direction of the 'Now on Sale' section for bed stuff. I could never understand how Kopek's mind worked, there were so many objects that were available to him in the bedroom, but he only ever chewed the bed and bedclothes. This restriction did not apply to books, of course, as he ate those at any and every opportunity. He didn't even bother with the two cushions that sat on the bed, as these were generally tossed onto the floor, slightly damp from dog slobber, but overall untouched. Everything else, the bed, the pillows, the duvet, the bed sheet, the mattress, and even the bed itself, which was made of wood, he would make a determined effort to shred. Although he did have a go at the rug in the bedroom once, there was very little damage, just a small chew on the corner. The rug mustn't have tasted very nice to his palate because he never bothered to chew it again. Apart from his toys, he has not once chewed any of his own possessions, not even his own bed that was then in the corner of our bedroom.

As far as Kopek and his creature comforts were concerned, there was a set routine for bedtime starting to emerge, and woe betide us if we ever deviated from it. First, we put the kettle on for a cup of coffee to take up to bed, and while this was boiling, we'd let Kopek out for his nightly constitutional. At the bottom of our garden, between the end of our fence and the garage, is where we park our campervan. Because of a combination of the size of the van, the angle of the road, we couldn't fit a gate between the fence and the garage. So I had rigged up a contraption to block the gap and keep Kopek contained, this involved some four by four lengths of wood, and chicken wire left over from making the rabbit run.

Most of the time, this was sufficient to keep Kopek from visiting our neighbour's gardens, which were accessible from the private road at the rear of our house. However, on the odd occasion when one of us has been to the garage and forgotten to put the 'gate' back properly (this must be Ronnie); this left the perfect space for

Kopek to go on an expedition. Occurrences during the day were a major headache, as that was when he visited the park, causing the phone calls at work. But in the evening, we were lucky in a small way, as for some reason he wouldn't stray far from the private road. If, when we let him out for his nightly pee and the way was open for him, there then ensued a night-time version of 'Catch the Hound.' This differed from the daytime version, in that as it was generally dark, he could see a lot better than me, and this gave him even more of an edge.

If Kopek hadn't returned by the time we'd made our coffee, then this was a sign that he was off exploring, and he didn't intend showing his face anytime soon. This meant I had to grab the torch; else the odds would be stacked far too much in his favour and set off down the back road. I would then attempt to find which lucky neighbour had the privilege of Kopek snuffling through their garden. It normally took me at least twenty minutes of playing 'The Game,' before Kopek decided he'd had sufficient enjoyment of proving to me that he was better at 'The Game' than I was. By this time, he thought it was time to go to bed. Just to add insult to injury, he normally beat me back to the house. Waiting for me in the bedroom, he'd give me a look as if to say, "What took you so long?"

As I've mentioned, both Ronnie and I are avid readers, so when we retire for the night, we normally read for half an hour or so before crashing. Ronnie always takes some digestives up to bed with her and includes two in the pile for Kopek. Ronnie would only give him his biscuits after she'd got into bed, so there was much pacing up and down the bedroom, Kopek's claws clicking on the wooden floorboards like a metronome beating time. After crunching his share, then hoovering up the crumbs, Kopek would hang around for a couple of minutes, just in case by some miracle another biscuit appeared. Kopek's personal ritual then follows; throwing himself down on his bed, chomping his lips, and sucking his teeth, trying to get at the last of the biscuit taste. Next, the big sighs start, huffing and puffing, some shifting around as he tries to get comfortable. Getting up and circling around, before throwing himself down again. We then have the pleasure of some more big sighs before he finally drifts off to sleep. He has recently added snoring to his delightful evening repertoire. I had never noticed before getting Kopek, how much like old people dogs were.

Along with the nightly ritual, there was a morning one starting, and this was when Kopek decided it was time for everyone to get up and take him to the field. The pacing and clicking of claws in a very un-soothing manner starts the routine. If this failed to wake us, he'd then shove his nose under the bed covers. As a tactic, this is quite successful, there's nothing quite like a cold, wet nose on some warm part of your body to wake you up in the morning. After about five minutes, he'd launch himself up, with his front paws landing on the window ledge. Resting there for a few minutes, he would watch the people passing by on the street below. At this point, we prayed that no dogs passed on their way to the field because if he saw another dog, the little whines started. After a few minutes of staring out of the window, he'd drop down from the window ledge, landing on the floorboards with all the grace of a pregnant elephant, and most of the same noise. The routine would then start again with the pacing. Ronnie seemed to be able to ignore all this, but I couldn't bear it, it started to irritate after two or three rounds. I'm sure that this was a game to him, but it was a battle of wills to me. His to see how long he could keep his routine up, and mine to see how long I could ignore it. Eventually, I could take no more, and I had to get up, and that meant that he'd won. I was not doing too well on the game stakes against Kopek. Perhaps it was time to think about carpeting the bedroom.

Chapter 6 - I hadn't killed him yet

It is truly amazing that Kopek was still alive. We'd considered dumping him on somebody's doorstep in a blanket, but one look at that daft face and big brown soppy eyes damn him.

Another time Kopek managed to get access to the upstairs, while in his bored mood, he decided most unusually to have a change from the usual bed munching, and instead worked his way through every other one of Ronnie's shoes. This seems to be a reoccurring theme with dogs. Every dog that I have ever had has eaten shoes at one point or another. What I really can't make my mind up about is, whether or not they only eat one of a pair on purpose, as it can't be just pure luck. Out of the six pairs of shoes that were in Ronnie's wardrobe, Kopek had eaten one of each of them. There was the odd tiniest of nibbles on some of the matching pairs, but I reckon he was just trying to work out which one of the pair tasted better.

Kopek went through a phase where his most favourite type of shoe to chew was cowboy boots. I love my cowboy boots and have worn them since I was sixteen. Not the same pair I hasten to add, but whenever one pair fell to bits, I would go out and get another pair as soon as possible. I'm never without at least one pair of boots and sometimes have had as many as three pairs at the same time. Around the time Kopek was thirteen or fourteen months old, I had two pairs of boots, one for everyday use, and another pair that were a bit smarter, that I would wear if we went out for dinner. To Kopek, cowboy boots must have been something special to him, because these were the only type of shoes that he took the time and effort to eat both pairs. The only other time he'd ever eaten a matching pair of shoes was my pair of suede slip-ons, and, to be honest, I think he was simply overwhelmed by the hideousness of them. After he had discovered cowboy boots, he never once bothered to eat any other type of shoe. Needless to say, as soon as he had had his little bit of fun with them, I would purchase another pair, but this was getting very expensive. Whenever I bought a pair, he would then spend the next few days hunting them out, and take great satisfaction in destroying them. This finding of boots seemed to become a challenge to Kopek. Unfortunately, these were one of the objects that I was far too often right when playing the 'Guess the Object' game. Whenever I came home to find the remains of both boots scattered around the house, he would be sitting there with that silly look on his face, it was almost as if he was saying "Look I found them, aren't you proud of me? Hiding them in that box behind the washing machine made them really tough to find, but I did it." My cowboy boots were, from then on, another thing I kept on top of the wardrobe, along with our books.

By the time Kopek had celebrated his first birthday, he had certainly grown into a most handsome dog. He had even pretty much grown into his ears and paws by then, but it didn't look like he was ever going to grow into that tongue, for that I will be forever grateful. We felt we should do something to mark the occasion, and Ronnie being ever the sentimentalist, made him a birthday cake out of Chappie. The 'cake' came complete with a candle, and it even had some 'icing' on the top. I'm not sure just how she achieved this, but obviously, it wasn't real icing.

Kopek was slowly maturing, there no longer seemed to be any discernable pattern to his destructiveness, but there was no doubt the frequency was reducing. A week or so might go by before he decided he was bored and needed something to occupy himself. It was around this time that I came home one day to find that the post had arrived while I was out, and Kopek hadn't eaten it. As he normally just couldn't help himself when it came to paper, this was an absolute first. He received an awful lot of praise that day, and I even gave him some extra treats, just to make the day memorable for him. He'd never received treats when I came home before, so I was hoping that this would make an impression, and he'd realise that good behaviour equalled treats.

His First Birthday

Kopek was an odd dog when it came to treats, when he was out on a walk he didn't seem bothered about them at all. However, when he was in the house, or even the pub, he would do anything for one. We only had to show him one, his bum would immediately drop to the floor, and he would then sit patiently like a model dog. Sitting was one of the things that Kopek seemed to do naturally, even when he was a pup, he would sit down on command. Although to be truthful, I'm not too sure he was actually sitting when he was younger, it was more of a fall than a sit, he just happened to fall on his bum. Out of all the commands he had learned, this was the most successful. He would even sit when out on the field, obviously not when he was careening around with another dog. But if he were just sniffing around, or even walking away, he would stop and sit when told, and almost always at the first time of asking.

Because of the way we had socialised Kopek and introduced him to lots of other dogs from a young age, he never showed any sign of aggression towards other dogs. Kopek took this behaviour to an extreme, and there were a few times where another dog took a dislike to him, but he didn't seem to realise it. There were one or two dogs on the field that were either very possessive of their balls (the one their owners would throw), or they were just plain grumpy. When Kopek raced over to say hello and see if they wanted to play, more often than not these dogs would growl at him, warning him away. If this didn't work, and it invariably failed, they would then try to chase him away being very vocal.

There were many occasions when Kopek just didn't realise that the other dogs were not happy and didn't want to play. He would run away when they barked at him, but within seconds, he would wheel back around and go back in for another go. I must admit, it was very rare that the other dog turned nasty, but if it did, I couldn't blame them. Kopek just seemed to keep pushing until he got a reaction. Unfortunately, it was often not the one he was after. Eventually, he would back off, and sulk about in the bushes for a while, until he spotted another dog to torment, hopefully, one that wanted to play.

There was one time when he showed a bit of aggression, and that was when there was this dog, a big bruiser of an Alsatian, which came charging across the field towards Ronnie. Kopek stopped his sniffing and stood almost as though he was at attention. As the dog got to within about twenty feet of Ronnie, Kopek went charging full speed straight towards it and knocked it off its feet. He then circled back to stand between Ronnie and the Alsatian, as if to say "Don't even try it pal, I'm watching you." A very uncharacteristic behaviour from him, but one that was in a way reassuring. From then on, I never worried about Ronnie being out on her own if she had Kopek with her.

On the list of favourite things to eat, were brushes, I think they came between paper and shoes. Kopek didn't seem to care what type, although I think he had a slight preference for the ones with proper stiff bristles. I lost count of the number of brushes we had to buy because he had found another one. We used a small hand brush to clean out the rodents once a week, as this proved the most useful way of cleaning their hutches. I think in the first three months of having Kopek, he managed to eat about twenty of these. The problem was that because of what we used the brushes for; we didn't want to leave them in the house. So we used to try to hide them in the garden somewhere and hope he wouldn't find them. There seemed to be three things that Kopek could find unerringly. The first was a book, the second my cowboy boots, and the third was a brush. Once I hid the brush in the blue bin, the one that you are supposed to put your paper waste in. That was a mistake, and I have to admit, it was not one of my brightest ideas. I'd let him out in the garden one afternoon when half an hour later, I noticed he hadn't come back in.

This was normally a very bad sign. At that time, if Kopek failed to let himself in after thirty minutes, it meant that he had found something to 'play' with, that or he was off playing down the field. I really should have thought it through. What were two of the things that Kopek found absolutely irresistible? Paper and brushes, and where in my wisdom did I choose to hide the brush? In the paper bin. Doh! I suppose it was a unique experience, I had never seen a paper covered garden before, it was sod's law that it was two days before the fortnightly collection, so the bin was pretty much full.

Thankfully, it was a calm day, but even so, the bits of paper seemed to have stuck in every bush and shrub. Cleaning up took me the best part of an hour and a half, but I would've finished a lot quicker if Kopek hadn't insisted on trying to help. As I gathered up piles of paper, he would dash in between my legs and steal some, then rush off to the garden with bits in his mouth. He did seem to lose his taste for brushes after his first year, he didn't stop eating them completely mind you, but they were no longer high on his list for some reason. That is unless I picked one up to brush the floor, and then he went into the same manic state as when we tried to vacuum.

About a week after the bin incident, I came home from work one morning, to find that Kopek had gone on one of his rampages. He was most definitely getting better in this regard, there were days that I would return home, and he was quiet as a mouse. Not a thing eaten or chewed, other days, however, were a completely different story. This had been one of those other days, and this was to be a pinnacle of his destructive behaviour. Not only had he found yet another book, thankfully one I had already finished reading, but he'd also decided to do some decorating. Great swathes of wallpaper had been stripped from the kitchen wall, up to about 7 foot high. Don't ask me, I have no idea how he managed to get that high, or how he got it off so cleanly, as it normally took me hours with a steamer to achieve the effect he had completed. A thin layer of paper covered the whole ground floor of the house, all of it shredded into the usual small wet chunks. The paper was from a combination of the wallpaper and the weekly free newspaper. The other little bit of alteration to the house décor was that he had decided to try his hand at carpentry and had chewed the moulding off the kitchen door frames up to about five foot from the ground. Why did he do this? I have no idea, but I do know he looked very pleased with himself.

Of course, we had to play the 'catch the hound' game, and throw him outside, before I could begin the task of cleaning up. Trying to clean up with Kopek helping didn't really work. So out he went, with me locking the door behind him, else he would have been back in within minutes. I cleared up the paper, and there was quite a lot of this because, for some reason, we'd had two free papers delivered that day. This was when I discovered he'd also tried his hand at carpet removal. I was just thankful this had not been one of those days he had managed to make his way upstairs. I dread to think what he would have got up to up there when he was in this kind of destructive mood. This was some kind of a record for Kopek. I'd only been out of the house for two hours, but the sheer amount of destruction was far out of proportion to the time he had been on his own.

As I may have mentioned, Ronnie was extremely house proud, and the continual eroding away of bits of it were starting to take its toll. While Kopek hadn't managed any major demolition in the house, there was a distinct air of untidiness around, and we were fighting a losing battle in keeping it spick and span. We'd bought an industrial carpet cleaner, and were now cleaning the carpets every month, but this was now making the carpet look worse by wearing it out. It was time to try to restore the house to some sort of habitable state. We thought we should at least do some damage limitation so that we didn't feel the need to keep apologising for the mess when visitors called round. Most of our friends thought it was great entertainment when they came round; they loved to hear the latest sagas that we'd been through. I had a sneaky feeling that they thought it was payback for when they came round when we had Tim.

It was time to replace the hall carpet, as there were more holes than actual carpet. It was a real shame because we'd been pleased with ourselves when we first bought it. Because the house was a 1930s build, we'd tried to buy furniture and fittings that were sympathetic to that period, and the carpet we'd chosen was a geometrically patterned one in a light colour. We hadn't even thought about getting a dog at that time, but I don't think we could have chosen a worse carpet if we had tried, at least as far as a dog proof one would be concerned. We decided to ditch the carpet idea; I don't think either of us could face the thought of Kopek destroying another carpet and elected to go for some sort of laminate flooring instead. At least, I thought rather selfishly; we could get a return on our investment by having hours of free entertainment watching Kopek slide up and down the hall.

We set off to B&Q; this made a nice change to the usual three shops that we had seemed to spend our lives in and looked around at what was available on our budget. There was no way we were going to buy anything that was overly expensive. Although we were confident that this would solve some of the issues with our problem child, we were by no means certain he wouldn't have a go at eating it. We weren't going to take the risk of paying for expensive parquet flooring just to have Kopek go on a chewing frenzy. We selected some flooring that was mid-range, with what looked like a simple interlocking fitting method. Despite my limitations when working with wood, I was determined that I would make a good job of this, so I was looking for something that would be simple to lay. Trying to lay a laminate floor in an 'L' shaped hallway is not easy, that is to say, it was not easy for me. It took me all weekend, but finally, it was down, and, what is more, it actually looked pretty good, even if I say so myself. The first thing Kopek did was pee on it. Why do they do that?

I once had a dog that was nine years old when I had to move house. He hadn't had an accident in the house for years, but the first thing he did on entering the new house was head straight to the lounge and have the longest pee I'd ever seen. Maybe it has something to do with them marking their turf. Whatever it is, I've never been impressed with it, and I was not impressed with Kopek then. After giving him a telling off, I cleaned up the pee and thought "Oh well, at least it's a lot easier than cleaning the carpet."

The next job on the list was to re-paper the kitchen wall, where Kopek had done such a sterling job of stripping it. We were lucky in that we still had a couple of rolls left over from when we first renovated the house. This is another thing that really irritates me, why in this period of computer controlled everything, can you never get the same colour of anything unless it happens to be in the same batch. While I concentrated on the wallpapering, Ronnie made a start on trying to do something with the kitchen table. She was very good with wood, unlike me, having completed a City and Guilds in carpentry. It didn't matter how many times I measured a piece of wood; it would never end up the size I needed it to be. That's why I was so proud of the rabbit run, and the laminate flooring, these are probably the only two wooden things that I've ever made, that actually stood the test of time. I must admit I was very impressed with how Ronnie fixed the corners; they almost looked as though that was how they were meant to be. It was only when you looked at the other two that you realised that something was amiss. We accomplished these two jobs quickly, and with little interference from Kopek, due to us locking him out in the back garden. There was no way I was going to attempt the wallpapering with him in the room, it just didn't bear thinking about, and I only had two rolls to play with.

The final job was to do something with the kitchen doorframes, as these were looking extremely tatty having been gnawed in an uneven manner. We thought it safer if Ronnie took on the job of reconstructing them. She mixed up some sawdust, along with a bit of wood glue, and then set about moulding the frames back into shape. I have to say that she did a fantastic job, so much so, that you would have been hard pushed to notice that there was anything wrong with them. Next up was the job of painting them with some white gloss. Overall, it took Ronnie almost three hours to complete the work on the doorframes, and when she'd finished, she stood back to admire her handiwork and the rest of the kitchen. Looking down she saw Kopek standing by her feet, looking with her into the kitchen. "See that. That's what it should look like." She said to Kopek "If you ever chew anything in here again, you'll be in so much hot water" She told him. It was just about then that she realised that while she'd been talking to him, Kopek had leaned against the doorframe and then slid down to the floor. Needless to say, she was less than happy about the furry doorframe that was the result of his leaning and sliding. "You little toad," she shouted at him. "Look at what you've done." Alarmed, Kopek jumped up and immediately backed into the opposite doorframe. I think we are the only house in the country with bespoke furry doorframes.

After we'd completed all this work on the house, it was time to have a big rethink about home-security for Kopek. We were both pretty tired of living with the dog gates. The resulting mayhem that sometimes ensued when Kopek decided he wanted to get through them was slowly wearing us down. I think it was that more than the sheer amount he cost us in repairs, that was getting to us so much. We discussed dog cages, as one or two of our friends had recommended them to us as an excellent way to control a dog left on their own, but with Kopek being such a big dog, we were not keen on that idea.

"What about a dog run of some sort?" I suggested to Ronnie.

"We'll never fit it in the house, and that will be worse than living with the gates," she replied.

"I was thinking it might be better suited in the garden."

"But what about if he started howling? I don't think that the neighbours would appreciate it." Although Kopek had calmed down a lot with regards to his howling, even ten minutes would be bad; he had a very loud howl.

"How about a run in the garage?" was my next brainwave. "That might work, we'll have to put in some light and heating, though, for when winter comes around."

We thought this might be a workable solution, so after some research on the Internet, we plumped for a professional dog run. The one we decided upon was ten foot long and five-foot wide, with a height of six and a half foot, we thought that this would be both big enough, and secure enough to keep even Kopek secured.

If you have ever put one of these together, you'll know that it's not an easy job. Because it was so big, I had to assemble it inside the garage, which left a foot of space around three sides, and about four foot on the final side where the gate was. Thankfully, it was supplied with real instructions, so it was easier in some ways than the infamous dog guard. Nevertheless, it still took me several hours to finally put together, due to the lack of space to work in. The sides simply bolted together, and then the chain-link fence was wrapped around the frame. Getting that chain link right was a long and tearful job, it had to be secured every few feet at the top and bottom with wire ties, and I am sure that these were specially designed to strip the flesh from fingers. Once finished, it was time to test it out with Houdini.

We put Kopek inside the run for about fifteen minutes to start with, just to see how he'd like it. He didn't like it at all. He howled for about ten of those minutes, and he kept clawing and biting the fence in a frantic bid for freedom. We persevered all weekend, continually putting him in for slightly longer periods at a time. By Sunday afternoon, we had worked up to leaving Kopek in his run for about an hour. We would put him in then watch television or read a book in the lounge while keeping an ear open for any howling, or sounds of destruction. The next stint was to be an hour and a half, but after fifteen minutes, there was a noise at the back door and in trotted Kopek. He was looking very happy with himself; he had managed to work loose one of the wire ties that secured the fence to the bottom of the frame. "Damn," I muttered to myself, now he knew he could get out he'd never stop trying. I was right, I had to double the number of wire ties just to keep the fence in place. What was worse was that he'd managed to work one of the corners loose, and somehow unlinked some of the fence to a height of about a foot. The result of this was that after every repair job, the run had a two-hour limit on how long it would keep Kopek imprisoned. He wasn't howling so much anymore, but that was because he was spending all his energy in endeavouring to escape.

By the time two weeks had passed, he'd managed to escape three times, he achieved this by worrying the original hole he had made in the fence and squeezing through. It didn't matter how much I repaired it; the time limits were steadily coming down. It was a battle I was slowly losing, he would escape, and I would repair the fence, but it got to the point that the run would only hold him for about forty-five minutes. This was becoming a very close race. Most of my meetings at work lasted for at least half an hour, and as it took me five minutes to get to and from work, it meant that I only had five minutes leeway. If I had a meeting longer than half an hour, then I could pretty much guarantee that Kopek would be off roaming the local field by the time I arrived home.

One of the things I was worried about was that Kopek had no road sense. He was fine when he was with us, always sitting and waiting at the side of the road, but off the lead was a different story. Although our road is quiet, it does get some traffic, and I was a bit concerned that a car might hit him on his way to the field. When I was younger and still living with my parents, I had a dog with no sense of danger regarding cars. He was a rescue dog; a Belgian Bouvier called Charlie, the size of a house but the temperament of a lamb. If you have never come across these animals, it is difficult to truly understand their power. In Belgium, the dogs were traditionally used to pull milk carts, and herd cows. They would keep the cows in check by launching themselves at them and knocking them over with their chests, no mean feat. Where I used to walk Charlie was a massive open field that backed onto the sand dunes, and separating the two was a busy coastal road. There was one occasion when Charlie went barrelling straight towards the dunes, with me urgently calling him back before he reached the road. Unfortunately, I wasn't successful in stopping him, and he went straight into the road. He ran straight into a passing estate car, luckily, he hit the car and not the other way round. The driver did an emergency stop and jumped out; he was a nice man and was full of concern about the dog. I was desperately trying to reassure him that Charlie was fine; I even pointed to him running happily over the dunes. The reason I was desperate was that the back of the man's car had a very accurate portrait of Charlie, in the form of a dent. Thankfully, the man hadn't noticed this, and I hope he doesn't read this book. This was the reason I was concerned about Kopek escaping, as he's not built as solidly as Charlie, I didn't think he would win a battle with a car.

I must admit, I was close to admitting defeat with the dog run when I had another one of my brainwaves. I didn't get them often, but when I did, they were usually either absolutely brilliant or an unmitigated disaster. This idea also meant finding a use for the old dog gates, which made it even more brilliant in my mind. I simply tied one of the dog gates over the hole, the one that Kopek was continually trying to expand, with a whole load of wire ties. Success! From then on although I had to check the run every week, just to keep on top of the wire ties, it managed to hold him for as long as necessary, and it had the added bonus of keeping him occupied as he tried to chew his way out. After that, every time I had to go into work for a meeting, I would pop him into his run, with his special outside bed, lots of water, and a bone and toy to keep him occupied. He wasn't happy, but he seemed to put up with it. I had finally won a battle with Kopek; I cannot tell you how happy that made me, even if it was a little childish.

Chapter 7 - Out and about

One of the best aspects of owning a dog is finding new open green places. Travelling with Kopek can add its own special entertainment.

The camper van we had bought was another vehicle off eBay; we had owned one previously, so we knew all the pitfalls to look for when buying one. It was small but generously kitted out, it had its own water supply, sink, small cooker with two gas rings, a large double bed, and even had a portable loo. Because it was self-contained, we could drive out further afield than in the car, and make ourselves comfortable wherever we went. Kopek loved the big old bus, and every time I opened the big sliding side door, he would leap in and refuse to get back out. Quite often, I had to leave him in there for an hour or so, while I potted about in the garden or the garage. It was as though he didn't trust us to slip out and not take him with us as if we would. One of the things we loved to do with Kopek was to go to dog shows, we were not overly keen on the serious competitions, but the ones run by rescue centres and charities proved to be lots of fun. Kopek was in his element at one of these shows, what with all those other dog bums to sniff, and to have to put his 'mark' down everywhere, he was very busy indeed. We did enter him in a couple of events, such as 'The Dog with the Waggiest Tail,' or 'The Most Handsomest Dog,' but he never managed to win anything. I could understand him not winning the Waggiest Tail competition, as he refused to give it one wag until we left the field. But in my completely unbiased opinion, he should have won the most handsome dog one. Not that we were that bothered, as it was just for fun and to raise money for the charity, although some of the owners took it all very seriously.

I do find animal charities irresistible, as I often get the chance to stroke and pet the animals, and I think most of them do a fantastic job and need as much support as they can get. I had joined a dog's charity about four years back while we had Tim and had sponsored a dog called Bongo. Bongo was a real rascally looking fella. I think he was some sort of Lurcher, with the wiry, scruffy kind of look to him. Each Christmas and Easter, and sometimes for what seemed no reason at all, I would get a letter from Bongo, and he would tell me all about what he'd been getting up to. Then one Christmas I received a letter from a dog named Pingy! What had happened to Bongo? Well, I wrote to the charity, and they informed me that sadly Bongo had passed away. I must admit I was a bit upset, as I had come to love Bongo. So they then just picked another dog at random to replace him as my adoptee. Now this put me in an awkward position, although I had nothing against Pingy personally, she was a Yorkshire terrier, and they're not my favourite breed of dogs. I tend to prefer larger breeds, and this was not a dog I would have chosen to adopt, I would have preferred the opportunity to choose my own dog. Needless to say, I have carried on with the adoption, but I have left instructions that should anything happen to Pingy, I want to pick the next one myself.

One place we had stopped at before we got the campervan was Leasowe Castle Hotel, in the town of Wallasey. This was generally only an overnight visit on our way back from visiting my dad. The Wirral coastline has some beautiful places on it, and as it was just across the river Mersey from Liverpool, it was quite handy for when we visited my dad who lives in Southport. We'd stopped here a couple of times before as it is dog-friendly, and it's a superb hotel that was originally built in 1592. On this occasion, we'd left Kopek in the room while we went and had some dinner, followed by a couple of drinks in the bar. When we went back to the room Kopek was fine, he was just lying on the bed, mournfully watching the television. He looked up with a face that said "it's about time, those quiz programmes are so boring. Where's my walk?" I duly took him for his said walk. He loved it when we stopped there, as there are plenty of grounds for him to run his legs off just outside the hotel.

The next morning after breakfast, during which we had again left Kopek in the room, we returned to find he'd had one of his 'sessions' with the bed. He had totally shredded the top sheet along with about a foot of the blanket that was lying on top. I must be honest, we stood there for about five minutes debating whether we could hide this, but in the end, we decided to own up. We went down to the front reception taking the damaged bedclothes, and dragging the culprit behind us. I must say, he wasn't showing any signs of remorse, and he was happily sniffing every nook and cranny that we passed on the way. The lady at the front desk was lovely, and after explaining what had happened, she said, "Oh well, that's what dogs do." We were both pleasantly surprised by this reaction. She said that she'd have a word with the manageress about how much the damage was going to cost us, and offered that we keep the top blanket. Now, Ronnie had been after one of these blankets for some time, so she almost snatched the lady's hand off at this offer. She'd been looking on the Internet to see where she could get one from, and the only place she could find were some industry suppliers based in America. While the blanket only cost about forty pounds, the delivery was going to cost another hundred, so she had decided against it. A week after the stay at the hotel, I received a phone call from them asking for twenty-five pounds for the cost of replacing the blanket, they had very kindly written off the cost of the sheet. About another week after that, I received a very nice letter, with my receipt in it, and a promise of a warm welcome the next time we stayed; this was even extended to Kopek.

Last summer we thought we would take a holiday in the UK, and get some use out of the campervan. We had only used it for short trips, long weekends, and overnight so far, and we fancied giving it a real long-term test. Also, as Kopek was getting older, he was getting more trustworthy at being left on his own. It had reached the point that several weeks could go by before he decided he needed some extra entertainment. So we thought that we could finally trust him not to wreck the campervan if he were left his own for a little while. We plumped for North Wales and decided to spend ten days travelling around the coast. Ronnie had never been to Wales, apart from a business trip to Cardiff, and I hadn't been since I was very young, when the family had holidayed in Anglesey. We were both really looking forward to it, and the added benefit of taking Kopek along with us added to the sense of fun. This was one of the reasons behind getting the campervan in the first place, because while we loved to holiday abroad, we missed the animals, so we thought that this was the perfect answer. We planned to go to Liverpool to see my dad, and then head straight for Caernarvon as the starting point. Starting from there, we thought we would miss out all the overly touristic places along the coast up to that point. On the Saturday afternoon we waved goodbye to my dad and set off, we had no idea at that point where we were going to spend the night, but that for us was part of the adventure.

With this being the first time we had taken the camper for any type of lengthy run, I was a little apprehensive as to whether it would be completely reliable. It was an old van, built in 1990, but it had only done seventy-odd thousand miles, and with a two point five diesel engine, it should have been fine. But you know how it is when you drive an older vehicle for the first time for any distance, you always worry whether there will be a water pipe that won't take the sustained pressure or something like that. As it was, I needn't have worried, the van drove superbly, even reaching sixty-five miles an hour on the duel carriageway quite comfortably. We were about forty miles from Carnarvon when Ronnie started looking at the map to see if there were any campsites close to the town centre. I didn't want to do more walking than was necessary. She found a perfect spot, one that was just a couple of hundred yards from the town centre, so she gave them a ring, and much to my delight, they had space for us. It was a delightful site, with rows of pitches terraced into a hillside. Had we not known better, we would never have guessed we were anywhere near a town, everything was so peaceful and quiet.

We had been camping with Tim before, so we already had a large screw in the ground spike with which to attach Kopek's lead to, this was to stop him wandering off and terrorising the other campers. What we didn't reckon on, was that Kopek would chew his way through his lead and set off exploring. We were relaxing in the campervan, having a deserved mug of coffee, while deliberating what to do with the rest of the afternoon. We were interrupted from our discussion by some squeals of laughter from some children nearby.

"Bloody kids," I mumbled, I'm not overly fond of them, especially on holiday. I have a theory that all children should be shipped off to the Isle of Wight until they are capable of having an adult conversation. Looking out of the window my head dropped, Ronnie knew this sign.

"What's he up to then?"

"Well," I said. "It looks like he's been swimming somewhere because he is now giving some children a shower."

As Kopek had a lot of fur, he could retain an awful lot of water. When he shook himself, anyone nearby may as well have gone for a swim, as they couldn't have got much wetter. The kids thought it was great fun, and their parents were thankfully, quite understanding. Having dragged Kopek back to the campervan, I threw him inside and hunted around for something that would serve as a lead. The only thing I could find was a towrope, this was just about the right length, and it was fairly substantial. "That should keep him restrained for a bit," I said to Ronnie while tying Kopek back up to his stake.

Carnarvon is one of the nicest towns I've visited, but unfortunately, it's not very dog-friendly, we couldn't find any pubs that would allow the Kopek inside. However, as it was warm, we didn't mind sitting outside and having a few relaxing jars. The next morning, we searched out an excellent general hardware store, one of those old-fashioned ones, which sell absolutely everything from screws to coal scuttles. It was there that we found a replacement dog lead (metal), and a five-foot length of chain to extend it to allow Kopek a bit more freedom when attached to the spike. As it was such a nice day, we thought we would do some sightseeing, so we took it in turns to look after Kopek while the other went to look at the castle. As castles go, it's quite impressive. After a late breakfast in the town, we took Kopek over the river, where there is an excellent walk to be had. My definition of 'excellent' is that it's not too long, and there is a pub at the end of it. Having exhausted Carnarvon's dog-friendly amenities by early afternoon, we decided to move on and see where we could get to for about four o'clock. We always like to arrive at a new place around that time. It gives us a bit of time to have a look around before deciding where to eat or drink.

I must admit, we were both very much taken with North Wales, the people were very friendly, and the scenery was spectacular. We stopped at quite a few of the towns and villages on the coast; Phwelli, Cricketh, and Abersoch. All of them delightful, especially the little café on the seafront at Cricketh, this served one of the best breakfasts I'd had in a long time. The only place I was not too fond of was Harlech, and that was because the town is at the top of a large hill. The only way to get there was walking up a one-in-four narrow bending road. After struggling up it, we were both very much in need of a beer at the pub at the top. It is no wonder that Harlech castle is in such good condition, as I can't see too many invaders being in much of a condition to do any effective attacking by the time they had climbed that road. Going down was a lot easier, but a bit more treacherous as we had imbibed of a few glasses by then. Kopek didn't help, as he was keen to get back to the campervan to have his dinner, so he was tugging me along.

After Harlech, we went inland to Welshpool, where we found an excellent little campsite, about two miles outside of the town. This was a really well-kept site, with all the verges nicely trimmed, and the flowerbeds were immaculate. The site even had a bar come restaurant just outside, but, unfortunately, this did not allow dogs. As there was nowhere else to eat, and we couldn't be bothered to drive into town, we thought we would nip over to the bar for some dinner and refreshments. Up to this point, Kopek had been on his best behaviour, and apart from that first afternoon in Carnarvon, he hadn't caused any trouble at all.

As we were only going to be gone an hour, we thought it would be safe to leave Kopek in the campervan, and as dusk was approaching, we left a light on for him in the back. As we were sitting in the nearly empty bar finishing off our after-dinner drinks, another couple came in with two children.

"That's a lovely dog you have," the mother said. "He really seems to enjoy himself." She was staying in the caravan parked opposite to our campervan and had been watching Kopek playing the fool earlier in the day.

"Yes," Ronnie answered. "He's only a puppy, so he's got loads of energy, too much sometimes."

"We said hello to him as we passed, he was howling his head off." One of the children said.

Ronnie and I both looked at each other; this was not good. When Kopek howled, it normally meant that destruction was not far behind. We both quickly finished off our drinks and made hastily for the door.

"What can he eat?" I asked Ronnie.

"It can't be much, I'm sure we put everything away before we left," She replied.

We spent the next ten minutes walking back to the campervan, reassuring each other that it would be all right. Everything looked OK from the outside, and in the dim light, we could see Kopek sitting calmly in the driver's seat in his usual position. However, as soon as I opened the side door I was completely smothered in feathers. We must have forgotten to put away the pillows, and in a smallish campervan, two pillows worth of feathers seems like an awful lot. They were stuck everywhere, to the ceiling, in the cooker, even the space over the cab. Of course, Kopek looked like a cross between a dog and a chicken. Ronnie went into the van to start cleaning up while I tried to calm Kopek down and stop him tearing off around the campsite leaving a trail of feathers in his wake, I was only partially successful. Eventually, he calmed enough for me to put him on his lead, and attach it to the dog spike; I then went in the campervan to help Ronnie. There was no way we were going to be able to clean this lot up, at least not without a vacuum, and as we didn't bring one with us, it was going to have to wait until we got back home. At that point, we simply bundled Kopek back into the campervan and went to sleep for the night.

We awoke early the next morning, and Ronnie kindly offered to get out of bed and put the kettle on for the morning coffee.

"Oh God," she said.

"What? What's wrong?" I asked somewhat concernedly.

"Just take a look at this" She motioned out of the window.

There across our pitch, the next one, and the one after that was a trail of feathers, it had rained in the night, and the feathers, instead of blowing away, had sunk into the ground. If you have been reading carefully, you will have noticed that I have not said the name of this site, and that's because I'm ashamed to say, we quickly forgot about the coffee, and simply drove off. There was no way that we would have been able to pick all those feathers up, so if the owner of that site is reading this, we are both very sorry.

One of the consequences of having a breed like Kopek is that it's not possible to go anywhere without being stopped by people admiring him. Almost everyone we met always asked what type of dog he was, this was normally after hazarding a few guesses, such as an Alsatian, or Husky. We then had to go through the "Actually he's a British-Inuit. It's a fairly new breed. A cross between...." This became so repetitive that we did consider getting him an extendable tag, one that people could just pull out and read. I supposed we shouldn't have complained, at least people were taking an interest in our dog, and they had plenty of complimentary things to say about him. It was just that it became a little tiring after a while. Especially when Ronnie and I were trying to have a conversation in the pub, and someone would interrupt with "That's a lovely dog, what is he?" It was OK the first couple of times, but sometimes it happened four or five times in one night. Thankfully, as most people know him now in our regular haunts, this doesn't happen too often, but if we go further afield, then it happens a lot.

We are really lucky to have a great pub close to where we live in our town. The pub is called the Greyhound and has two bars plus an area out the back with plenty of seating. Being one of those rare pubs that welcome dogs inside, it's very popular with the local dog-owning fraternity. One day, I counted as many as twelve dogs inside and outside of the pub. This, of course, is not without its problems, as having so many dogs in one place is simply asking for trouble. There have been several occasions, when people have lost their drinks off the table, due to two or more dogs getting over excited. Nevertheless, the staff at the pub are very friendly, and very accommodating about the dogs, they don't seem to mind the trouble they cause. Kopek really comes into his own when we're at the pub, as he's generally so well-behaved. The only time he acts up is if he spots another dog too close by, then he will whine a little and want to go over and play. But even then, after a few minutes, he'll just settle down again.

It was at this pub that Kopek first developed his taste for Guinness. You may have guessed by now that I like my Guinness, and in fact, I very rarely drink anything else, unless I found myself in a pub that didn't sell it. Ronnie and I generally go out for a couple of drinks once or twice during the week, and again at the weekend. We always take Kopek with us when we go to the pub, and for every pint I have, I'll let him have three fingers. That's to say, that I dip a finger in my pint and let him lick it off, then repeat this twice more, and he certainly grew to love it. Whenever I come back from the bar with a pint in my hand, he'll keep pestering me until he gets his bit. If I come back to our seat having been to the loo, he looks around as if to say, "Where's my Guinness then?"

When we take him to the pub, we always bring along the length of chain so we can extend his lead when we sit outside. This gives him enough freedom to mooch around the table while being short enough to keep him out of too much trouble. One day we had gone there on a Sunday afternoon, and because it was such a bright sunny day, we sat outside on one of the wooden trestle tables. There were two other dogs outside that day, and Kopek was stretching his neck trying to get as close to them as possible. While I was talking to a chap at the next table, he was asking what sort of breed Kopek was, Kopek stood up on the bench seat, with his eyes fixed on the other two dogs. I'd half turned around to tell him to get down, when quick as a flash that super-sized tongue of his was in my pint. He drank about a third of it before anyone could react. Needless to say, he was not allowed any more to drink for the rest of the afternoon. It wasn't long before the Guinness started to take effect, at first, he seemed fine, and then he started slowly to sway from side to side. He then sat down for a moment, looking round at his backside, as if to say, "How did that happen?" Eventually, he gave up the struggle, flopped down, and went to sleep for the next hour or so.

That experience by no means deterred him from his drinking habits, and in fact, he will still try to steal my pint at any opportunity. It wasn't just my pint if ever anyone were careless enough to leave theirs within his reach; he'd have a quick slurp. I've lost count of the number of replacement pints I've had to buy. Everyone at the pub soon became used to Kopek, and some of the regulars love to play with him when they arrive, before going in for their drinks. Many people would walk up and make a fuss of him, talking to him in that way that people do to dogs, they would then say hello to us and go into the pub. One day I had occasion to walk through the pub on my own without Kopek in tow, and I couldn't believe it, apart from the barman, not one person said hello to me. It was as though they didn't recognise me without Kopek. It's a sad day when people in your own local know your dog more than they know you. Kopek has become such a popular regular at that pub that he now has his own stainless steel water bowl.

Another pub that we have been to a fair bit is the Butt and Oyster; this is in a small village called Pin Mill. This is a marvellous old pub, which sits right on the river Orwell, making the views spectacular. It serves great food, and also allows dogs, but only in the bar area. We turned up there one Sunday in early autumn, with our friend Chris, and two of his younger daughters, and we were hoping to get an early lunch. I went up to the bar to order the drinks, and food and the barman asked where we would be sitting.

"In the window seat, just over there," I replied.

"Oh, I'm sorry," he said, "We don't allow children in the bar area."

"Ah, I don't suppose you allow dogs in the restaurant either," I asked.

"I'm afraid not," he confirmed. What to do? I went back over to Ronnie and Chris.

"We can't eat in the bar because of the kids, and we can't eat in the restaurant because of Kopek," I told them. There was a moment's silence, which was broken by my suggestion of "I don't suppose you'll put the kids in the car would you?" Chris just looked at me, shaking his head; he was well used to my attitude towards children by then. I'm afraid the older I get, the lower my tolerance of children drops, I really do prefer animals to children, or even most people for that matter. The barman relented by saying "As it's early, and there's no one else in, if you eat quickly I'll let you stay in the bar," saving us from this dilemma. "But if anyone complains, you'll have to take the children outside." We thanked him, and duly wolfed down our lunches.

We have recently found another pub, not far from the Butt and Oyster, that allows both children, and well-behaved dogs in the bar area. This is the Freston Boot, which is in, believe it or not, Freston. This is another small village near Pin Mill, and it has the advantage of being closer to home that the Butt and Oyster. It also has a large grassed outside area with trestle tables; this allows us to let Kopek off the lead if there is no one else around. I can heartily recommend the food in this pub; it's just how you would imagine good home cooked fare to be. It may not be on the river like the Butt and Oyster, but out the back, it has fantastic views of the Orwell Bridge spanning the river.

Yet another pub we enjoy is the Dove. I'm sure you have realised by now, that Ronnie and I somewhat relish our visits to pubs. This is a lovely pub just on the outskirts of the town centre. Again, the landlord and landlady allow dogs both in the bar and out in the courtyard. The Dove holds beer festivals at various times throughout the year, and although I only ever drink my Guinness, both Ronnie and Kopek, are partial to a bit of real ale every now and then. In addition to the beer, Kopek is really appreciative of the landlady's barbecues, or more specifically the food she cooks on them.

As I write this today, Kopek has just reached his eighteen-month birthday. He has just started to reach his adolescence period I think, as he is starting to show a bit more confidence with other dogs, and not running away if they have a go at him. He's not aggressive, but he is standing up for himself a bit more. Last week was a very proud moment for us all. He tried to mount Miya for the very first time; there were almost tears in my eyes as I thought, "You've become a man my son." This is not something that we want to encourage, but I was beginning to think that he might be a bit odd, as he had shown no interest in that sort of thing up to this time.

I have to pinch myself sometimes, just to make sure that I'm not dreaming, and he is really only eighteen months old. I cannot believe how much he has done in his short life. Neither Ronnie nor I can wait to see what fun he gets up to in the next eighteen months. Moreover, we must be mad because we are thinking about getting Kopek a friend to play with; we are hoping it might cure him of his boredom and resultant destructiveness. But it probably won't, and with our luck, we'll end up with another just as bad. However, that's dogs for you, and neither of us would have any different.

Sadly, we have recently lost Donald and Wayne, both of them to some animal I fear. Oddly enough, there was absolutely no sign of any disturbance, but their hutch was open when I went to feed them in the morning, and they were gone. I did find a small hole in the wire in one corner of the run, but again there was no evidence of any animal. Ronnie, of course, chooses to think that they simply decided to go off on their travels, and she awaits a postcard from some far-flung place. She reluctantly agreed to dismantle the run, and although this now gives Kopek more space, it does make the garden look a bit empty. So we are now down to just Kopek, and Gucci, but they continue to do their utmost to keep us entertained.

I feel I should end this with a word of warning. Owning a dog like Kopek, and that includes any of the 'Northern' type breeds, is a lot of hard work. They are not a breed for the novice dog owner. While having a fantastic temperament, they are all very stubborn and single-minded, training one is a real challenge. Despite how cute they look as puppies, please do your research before embarking on the life of destruction you will almost certainly have. The rescue centres are full of these types of dogs, where novice owners just can't keep up with them. However, if you do decide to get one, then you will find that they have so much to give back. For Ronnie and me, they are the perfect dogs, and despite, or maybe because of his antics, we wouldn't swap Kopek for any other animal.

Kopek's Story in Pictures

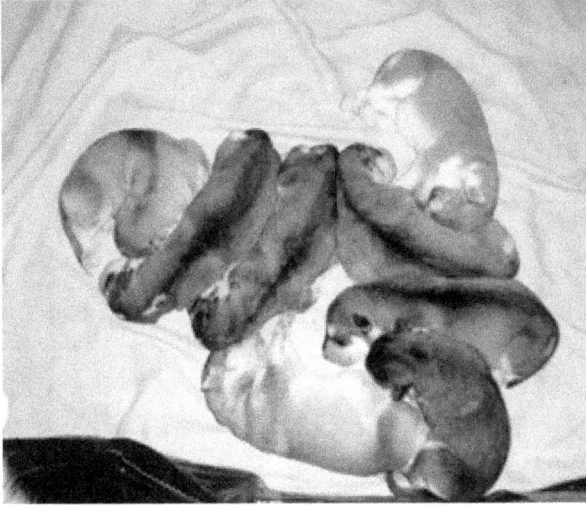

Kopek and his siblings a few days' old

Small and Spiky (he's on the left)

The Tongue

The New Arrival

One Year Old

Kopek with his Friend

A Proud Dog

The First Time in the Snow

Daft as a Brush

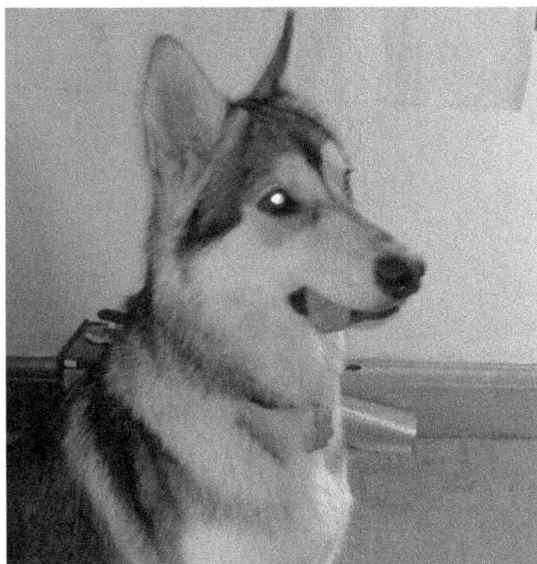

Still Doesn't Quite Fit

www.ingramcontent.com/pod-product-compliance
Lightning Source LLC
LaVergne TN
LVHW021133080426
835509LV00010B/1342